PRESERVED LOCOMOTIVES
Fifth Edition

H. C. Casserley

LONDON

IAN ALLAN LTD

First published 1967
Fifth edition 1980

ISBN 0 7110 0991 0

© Ian Allan Ltd 1980

Published by Ian Allan Ltd, Shepperton, Surrey; and printed by Ian Allan Printing Ltd at their works at Coombelands in Runnymede, England

ADDENDA

Tiny, South Devon Railway, moved to Dart Valley Railway museum.

No 5051 *Dryswllyn Castle/Earl Bathurst*, GWR 4-6-0, nameplates to be carried for set periods each year.

No 7754, GWR 0-6-0PT, on loan to the Llangollen Railway from the National Museum of Wales, to whom it was donated by the NCB.

No 13809, S&DJR 2-8-0, is to go to the Midland Railway Trust, Butterley.

No 30499 SR 4-6-0 is to be preserved by the Urie S15 Locomotive Preservation Group.

No 31638, SR 2-6-0, is to be preserved on the Bluebell Railway.

No 34027 *Taw Valley*, SR 4-6-2, is to be preserved on the North Yorkshire Moors Railway.

No 48518, LMS 2-8-0, is to be preserved on the proposed Peak Park Railway.

No 70000 *Britannia*, BR 4-6-2, is to be transferred to the Nene Valley Railway.

No D5705, BR Class 28 Co-Bo, is to be preserved by the Diesel Traction Group.

No D1015 *Western Champion*, BR Class 52 C-C, is to be preserved by the Diesel Traction Group.

Ex-industrial locomotives

Bagnall (2898/1948) 0-4-0F to the North Road Museum, Darlington.

Hunslet (3180/1944) 0-6-0ST *Antwerp* on loan to the North Yorkshire Moors Railway.

Hunslet (3782/1953) 0-6-0ST *Arthur* to Quainton Road.

Peckett (1438/1916) 0-4-0ST to Swindon & Cricklade Railway Society.

Sentinel (6807/1928) 0-4-0TG *Gervase* into store.

Foreign locomotives

Scwarzopf, Berlin (9124/1927) 0-4-0WT *Bronhilde* to Sittingbourne (1ft 11½in gauge).

Contents

Introduction   3

Abbreviations   6

Part One
Locomotives built between 1813 and the 1850s   7

Part Two
Locomotives built for Public and Passenger Carrying Railways from the 1860s   17

Part Three
Industrial Locomotives from the 1860s

Part Four
Foreign or British-exported Locomotives   166

Index of Industrial and Light Railways' Locomotives   170

Index of Foreign Built Locomotives   185

Principal Centres of Preserved Locomotives   187

Photo Credits   189

Index   190

Introduction to the First Edition (1967)

This first edition of a book of *Preserved Locomotives* is intended to describe briefly and to illustrate all locomotives which have over the years survived the breakers' yard or scrap dealer and been retained in one form or another either in museums or under private ownerships.

With the standard gauge steam locomotive now completely extinct on British Railways, interest in preservation has never been so widespread as it is at the present time, and apart from numerous appeals for funds to purchase examples of some of the last types to run on British Railways, one reads almost every month of smaller locomotives, usually industrial engines owned by private concerns, being purchased by various individuals for display on their own premises, often in gardens and consequently not generally on public view.

Apart from the various specimens preserved in the past and now to be found in many museums all over the country, including of course the fine collections accumulated by British Railways and exhibited at Clapham,* York and Swindon, with many more at present laid aside awaiting restoration and eventual display, there are the activities of the various preservation societies which have grown up in recent years to maintain lengths of line in operational condition with locomotives in running order.

The first of these was the Talyllyn Railway, that small and delightful narrow gauge line in Wales, running through magnificent scenery, threatened with closure in 1950 after an existence of 85 years, and worked throughout that period by its two original engines. To save it from extinction a band of enthusiasts got together and through the heroic efforts of the members managed to raise sufficient funds to keep the little railway running, only made possible by their many hours of voluntary unpaid labour which they were prepared to devote towards this worthy purpose. This valiant initial effort was soon taken up by another Society formed to re-open the Festiniog Railway, which in this case had lain derelict for a few years. Here again the much needed financial support and labour were forthcoming, and like the Talyllyn, it is now established on a permanent

basis, with more newly acquired locomotives, and with extension in progress with the ultimate object of reaching Blaenau Ffestiniog once more, originally the upper terminus of the line.

These two inaugural efforts have since been followed by others, the Welshpool & Llanfair, another narrow gauge line, and some standard gauge lines in other parts of the country; the Bluebell Railway, the Dart Valley Light Railway, Keighley & Worth Valley, Severn Valley Railway, and others. Not all of these have at present been able to restore passenger carrying trains over their lines, but hope to be in a position to do so in 1968.

All of them have obtained specimens of locomotive classes which would otherwise already have become extinct, and these therefore come undoubtedly within the definition of preserved locomotives, notwithstanding they are still maintained in running order, as distinct from static exhibits in museums and the like.

Going back to the earliest times, it is perhaps somewhat remarkable that so many of the first steam locomotives escaped destruction in the earlier part of the 19th century, although there are some bad gaps.

It is perhaps hardly surprising that the very first locomotive to run on rails, Trevithick's engine in 1804, was lost in obscurity, but there are fortunately three early engines in existence which predated the well known *Locomotion* and *Rocket*, both of which are instinctively and at first thought imagined to be the earliest locomotives (many of the uninitiated even think that they were the first steam engines, but in fact some 30 had already been built before the appearance, in 1825 of Stephenson's *Locomotion,* now to be seen at Darlington station).

The earliest of all is Hedley's *Wylam Dilly* of 1813, now to be seen in the Royal Scottish Museum, Edinburgh, and as the oldest locomotive in existence takes pride of place as the first subject for description and illustration. It was followed by *Puffing Billy* in 1814, now in the Science Museum, Kensington, and the Hetton Colliery locomotive of 1822 which reposes at York.

These early years until the later 1840s are very well covered indeed in the circumstances, and examples of most of the general types of design which were evolved during that period have survived, about 15 in all.

*Clapham of course now closed and the collection disposed, mainly to York.

After 1850 however there is a bad period. By that time railways had become well established and lost their novelty, and for the next half century practically nothing was done in the way of preservation. Such examples as we have of engines of that period, and they are considerable in number, are of long lived classes which lasted until comparatively recent years.

There are however inevitably some regrettable gaps such as a Sharp single, a 2–2–2, which became numerous in the 1850s and was used on many railways. A good example of one of these, from the old Shrewsbury & Chester Railway, which became Great Western No 14, built in 1848 and withdrawn in 1885, was in fact stored until as late as 1920, and then unaccountably and unforgivably cut up. The GWR were particular sinners in this respect; they had also preserved their famous broad gauge engines, the original *North Star* and *Lord of the Isles* at Swindon for many years, and suddenly, with a single act of ruthlessness scrapped them in 1906. True they later atoned for this in some respect by building a full sized replica of *North Star* for the Darlington Centenary Exhibition in 1925, and this is still to be seen, but the only genuine broad gauge engine left is the little *Tiny* on Newton Abbot platform, hardly a typical example of this remarkable era.

These are not the only examples of locomotives preserved and later scrapped. The LMS was very naughty in this respect in 1932 when it decided that three Midland engines, together with a North London 4–4–0T, which it had restored in 1930 with a view to preservation, were not to be kept after all. Whether by coincidence or otherwise it must be remarked that this happened shortly after the arrival of Sir William Stanier at Derby, and that eminent engineer had come from Swindon!

These regrettable occurrences could and should have been avoided, but there are still other milestones in the locomotive history of this country which we can only deplore.

A Webb compound, although an unsuccessful design, was an interesting link in LNWR history, and in later years a 'Precursor' or 'George the Fifth' (*Sirocco* which lasted until 1948 might well have been saved by the newly formed British Transport Commission). What about such a famous engine as *Cardean* of the Caledonian? A Great Eastern 'Claud' would also be very desirable, the 'Decapod' would have been impracticable in any case, as it had been so entirely rebuilt and transformed, but Midland No 2290 should not have been scrapped, and a representative Garratt, the Gresley or one of the LMS ones, would fill a notable gap.

However, one could go on indefinitely, but before leaving the sad subject of the 'might have beens' one can only regret that whilst nearly all of the major pre-Grouping companies are represented there is nothing from the old Manchester, Sheffield & Lincolnshire, or London, Chatham & Dover, there is no Cambrian (unless one counts the Welshpool & Llanfair), no Hull & Barnsley, no modern

Below: International steam on the Nene Valley Railway as German 2–6–2T No 64.305 and Danish B class 4–6–0 leave Wansford station.

Furness, no M&GNJR, no Barry or Rhymney (there are very few from the numerous South Wales companies) whilst the Glasgow & South Western is poorly represented.

But we must be thankful for what we have.

There are so many fine specimens of bygone days still to be seen up and down the country if one knows where to look for them, and it is hoped this book may be some guide to their whereabouts.

Introduction to Fifth Edition   1980

The first edition of this series appeared in 1967 and its 12-year old introduction has been retained to depict the scene when this series was first introduced. Since that date there have been innumerable developments in the preservation scene and many additional locomotives have joined the ranks of those saved for posterity. These have been acquired by various organisations, some of them new to the ranks, under various schemes which have come into being. There have also been many changes of location and ownership, all necessitating widespread revision and amendment.

The supply of main line steam locomotives would long since have dried up but for the enterprise of Woodham Brothers, scrap breakers, of Barry in South Wales, who had the foresight to purchase over 200 engines from BR and set them aside. Many of them (98 as at early 1979) have indeed been acquired by various preservation bodies and over 20 have been restored to working order, after the expenditure of much time and energy, mostly on a voluntary basis, and of course the very considerable problems of finance. Meanwhile most of the remainder (119 in all, including 2 diesels), have been exposed to the elements for 12 years or more, have badly deteriorated and are in a poor state, although some are still earmarked for possible resuscitation.

However, no main line locomotives, the survivors of which are chiefly of GWR origin, with a few BR, LMS or SR types, now remain of classes of which there are not examples already preserved.

In the industrial field the position is much the same, as although steam locomotives are still to be found in use here and there, to a rapidly dwindling degree, they are mostly of more modern types, particularly the ubiquitous Austerity saddle tanks of wartime design. Recent acquisitions of this type have indeed made them numerically the most preserved class, approaching nearly 50 examples in all, exceeding the Hunslet 0–4–0ST quarry engines which previously occupied this position.

Another development on a small scale has been the importation of foreign built engines from overseas, dealt with in a separate section, which is new since the first appearance of the book in 1967.

Perhaps the most startling development since the first edition however, and which few could have foreseen at the time, has been the preservation of main line diesel locomotives, which had done so much to hasten the demise of the steam engine. Profiting from the lessons of past experience, and taking a broad view of the future, it has been accepted that railway locomotive preservation should not necessarily come to an end with the steam era, and that a representative selection of diesels (and electrics for that matter) should continue the story. Even so, the realisation came too late to save either of the two pioneer main line diesel electric locomotives in the country, LMS Nos 10000 and 10001, the first of which appeared in December 1947, just before Nationalisation.

Even 12 years ago it was not fully appreciated that intensive usage would give diesel locomotives a short life span by comparison to steam locomotives. In some cases this has been in the nature of 15 to 20 years, compared with anything up to half a century, often much more, of its predecessors.

Back in 1967 it would have seemed most unlikely that some of these earlier diesels were to see such comparatively early extinction, which has in fact happened, and even if it had there would have been few anxious to perpetuate their memory. Now the 'Westerns' for instance, already an extinct class on BR, achieved such widespread acclaim that no less than six examples have been preserved, some on private lines in working order.

There are consequently several new pages in this edition devoted to main line diesel and electric classes. As in prevous issues it is not possible in a book of this size to cover the several hundred industrial petrol driven and diesel locomotives, apart from one or two selected examples of unusual or outstanding interest. The industrial section is confined to steam locomotives, listed under the individual makers' lists, and the author has endeavoured to include all known steam locomotives within this category, complete as far as is known up to December 1979, but here again the position is constantly fluid, especially as regards changes of ownership and location. Owing to the time lag between compilation and publication there is incidentally a small amount of information which has become out of date, for which the reader's indulgence and understanding is appreciated. By the very nature of things the position cannot be static and unchanging.

Illustrations of individual locomotives have necessarily, by reason of space, to be confined to a few representative examples of the principal makers, and more particularly any of unusual interest. Principal dimensions are also included, where available, but these are sometimes difficult to obtain in the case of engines in private ownership.

Unlike most other books dealing with the subject of preservation, which usually give brief details of the engines which are to be found at the numerous locations around the country, this volume deals with the subject from an entirely different angle. All main line engines are represented by an illustration of each class (of which in some cases there are several representatives) with particulars of origin, history and background.

The order of presentation is in building date order of the first appearance of each class described, although this is not necessarily or even usually the year of construction of the actual engines which have survived.

It should be noted that not all the National Railway Museum's collection of locomotive and carriages are on view at any one time.

Berkhamsted

H. C. Casserley
January 1980

General abbreviations

B&NCR	Belfast & Northern Counties Railway	LMS	London, Midland & Scottish Railway
BCDR	Belfast & County Down Railway	LMS(NCC)	London, Midland & Scottish Railway (Northern Counties Committee)
BP&GVR	Burry Port & Gwendraeth Valley Railway	LNER	London & North Eastern Railway
BR	British Railways	LNWR	London & North Western Railway
CDR	County Donegal Railway		
CR	Caledonian Railway	LSWR	London & South Western Railway
D&SER	Dublin & South Eastern Railway	LT&SR	London, Tilbury & Southend Railway
G&SWR	Glasgow & South Western Railway	MNR	Manx Northern Railway
GCR	Great Central Railway	MR	Midland Railway
GER	Great Eastern Railway	NBR	North British Railway
GNR	Great Northern Railway	NER	North Eastern Railway
GNR(I)	Great Northern Railway (Ireland)	NLR	North London Railway
		NSR	North Stafford Railway
GNSR	Great North of Scotland Railway	S&DJR	Somerset & Dorset Joint Railway
GS&WR	Great Southern & Western Railway	S&DR	Stockton & Darlington Railway
GWR	Great Western Railway	SE&CR	South Eastern & Chatham Railway
IoMR	Isle of Man Railways		
L&MR	Liverpool & Manchester Railway	SER	South Eastern Railway
		SR	Southern Railway
L&YR	Lancashire & Yorkshire Railway	W&LLR	Welshpool & Llanfair Light Railway
LBSCR	London, Brighton & South Coast Railway		

Part One

'Wylam Dilly' 0–4–0

1813

Driving wheels: 3ft 3in (4 coupled, spur driven via central crankshaft)
Weight: 8 tons (engine), 4 tons (tender)
Cylinders: 9in x 36in
Pressure: 50lb

The earliest engine in existence, and one of the first ever built. Constructed by William Hedley, assisted by Timothy Hackworth, in 1813 at Wylam Colliery, Northumberland. Because of the original weak cast-iron plateway, the engine was rebuilt in 1815 as an eight-wheeler, but altered back to a four-wheeled arrangement in 1830, when the line was relaid. In 1862 the engine went to Craghead Colliery. On withdrawal it was presented to the Royal Scottish Museum, Edinburgh, where it can now be seen. In 1822 *Wylam Dilly* had its rail wheels temporarily replaced by a pair of paddles. The whole contraption was mounted in a small boat to convey coal barges. Thus it was an early steam tug too.

'Puffing Billy' 0–4–0

1814

Driving wheels: 3ft 3in
Weight: 8¼ tons
Cylinders: 9in x 36in
Pressure: 50lb

Hedley's second engine for the Wylam Colliery was built in 1814, a year after *Wylam Dilly*. Like its predecessor, it was rebuilt in 1815 as an eight-wheeler to spread the load over the weak plateway, but reconverted in 1830, in which form it ran until 1862, when it was acquired by the South Kensington Museum. The illustration is an interesting photograph taken when the engine was still at work more than 100 years ago.

Hetton Colliery 0–4–0 1822

Driving wheels: 3ft 0in
Weight: 9¾ tons (including tender)
Cylinders: 10¼in × 24in
Pressure: 80lb

Built in 1822 by George Stephenson and Nicholas Wood at the workshops of Hetton Colliery, Durham, one of the engines constructed for working the eight-mile line between the colliery and the coal staithes on the River Wear. Rebuilt in 1857 and again in 1882. Withdrawn from service in 1912 and preserved, later going to York Museum. It was transferred to Beamish Museum, Durham in 1974. It led the procession of engines at the Darlington Centenary Exhibition in 1925.

S&DR 0–4–0 'Locomotion No 1' 1825

Driving wheels: 4ft 0in
Weight: 6½ tons
Cylinders: 9½in × 24in
Pressure: 50lb

George Stephenson's celebrated engine for the Stockton & Darlington Railway was built in 1825. It was not of course, by any means the first steam locomotive, the honour of building must go to Richard Trevithick, who in 1804 had constructed the first engine to run on rails. Stephenson himself had moreover previously built 10 engines for colliery work, and there were others, but *Locomotion No 1*

was the first to operate on a public passenger carrying line. The engine was preserved on a pedestal at Bank Top station, Darlington as illustrated, but has been removed to the museum at Darlington North Road. A full scale working replica was built to take part in the 1975 150th Anniversary celebrations at Shildon.

T. Hackworth 0–4–0 'Sanspareil' 1829

Driving wheels: 4ft 6in
Weight: 4 tons
Cylinders: 7in × 18in

A contestant in the 1829 Rainhill Trials, built by Timothy Hackworth. Unfortunately it was excluded from qualifying for the prize (won by Stephenson's *Rocket*) owing to being slightly over the maximum permitted weight. It later ran on the Bolton & Leigh Railway, and in 1844 was put to work as a stationary boiler at Coppull Colliery, Chorley, where it remained until 1863. It is preserved in the Science Museum, South Kensington.

Stephenson 0–2–2 'Rocket'

Driving wheels: 4ft 8½in
Weight: 4¼ tons
Cylinders: 8in × 17in
Pressure: 50lb
Tractive effort: 825lb

Probably the best known of all the famous early locomotives, George Stephenson's engine of 1829 was built for the Rainhill Trials, at which it proved an easy winner. It worked on the Liverpool and Manchester Railway until 1836, when it was sold out of service, subsequently coming into the hands of the Brampton Railway, a small line in Cumberland, where it worked until 1862. The cylinders were at first steeply inclined at an angle of about 45°, but it was at some period rebuilt with almost horizontal cylinders in which condition the original engine is preserved at the Science Museum. A full-sized replica of the engine in its original condition was built by Stephenson & Co for the LMS, and exhibited at its 1930 Centenary Exhibition at Liverpool as shown in the picture. A working replica has been constructed for the 1980 celebrations of the Rainhill Trials.

Shutt End Railway 0–4–0 'Agenoria'

1829

Driving wheels: 4ft 0½in
Weight: 11 tons (including tender)
Cylinders: 8½in × 36in

Built in 1829 by Foster Rastrick & Co of Stourbridge, for the Earl of Dudley's Shutt End Colliery Railway, Kingswinford, Staffordshire. It was almost identical to the *Stourbridge Lion* built in 1828 by the same firm, which was sent to America and was the first locomotive over there to run on rails. *Agenoria* worked until about 1864. It was for many years on exhibition in the Science Museum, Kensington, but has now been moved to the National Railway Museum, York.

Canterbury & Whitstable Railway 0–4–0 'Invicta'

Driving wheels: 4ft 0in
Weight: 6¼ tons
Cylinders: 10in × 18in
Pressure: 40lb

Built in 1830 for the Canterbury & Whitstable Railway, on which line it worked until about 1839. At present under restoration at York, but will probably return in due course to its permanent home in Canterbury.

Killingworth Colliery 0–4–0 'Billy'

Believed to have been built about 1830 by Robert Stephenson & Co, but the exact date is uncertain. It seems to have carried the name *Billy* at some period. It ran on the Killingworth Wagonway, being rebuilt in 1867, until 1881, when it was presented to the City of Newcastle by Sir Charles Mark Palmer. It was placed on a pedestal at the north end of the High Level Bridge until about 1896, when it was moved to the platform at the Central station. In 1945 it was transferred to the Municipal Museum, Newcastle. This engine has sometimes been erroneously referred to as *Puffing Billy,* but it has no connection with the engine of that name in the Science Museum.

GWR 2–2–2 'North Star'

Driving wheels: 7ft 0in
Weight: 23 tons 7 cwt
Cylinders: 16in × 16in

Mention must be made of this historic loco-motive, although unfortunately what is to be seen today is not the original, but a replica built in 1925. The old engine was one of the earliest and best known of the GWR broad gauge. It was one of two built in 1837 by R. Stephenson & Co for the New Orleans Railway of the USA but never delivered. Constructed to a gauge of 5ft 6in, it was converted to 7ft 0in and purchased by the GWR and named *North Star*. It was reboiled in 1854 and worked until 1871. On withdrawal it was preserved at Swindon, but was broken up in 1906. The replica was built for the Stockton and Darlington's centenary in 1925 and is preserved in Swindon Museum.

L&MR 0–4–2 No 57 'Lion'

Driving wheels: 5ft 0in
Cylinders: 12in × 18in
Pressure: 50lb
Tractive effort: 2,160lb

An early engine of the Liverpool & Man-chester Railway, built by Todd, Kitson & Laird in 1838 it was L&MR No 57, and later became the LNWR's No 116. On withdrawal from active service in 1859 it was purchased by the Mersey Docks and Harbour Board for use as a stationary boiler. In this humble capacity it worked for many years, unknown to the rail-way world at large. Fortunately, when the

question of its replacement came about in the 1920s it was 'discovered' and brought to the notice of the LMS authorities, who purchased it and restored it to its original condition in working order. Since then it has been in steam on several occasions, and was used in the filming of *The Titfield Thunderbolt*. The illustration shows it at Dunchurch in 1961.

LNWR 2–2–2 No 49 'Columbine' 1845

Driving wheels: 6ft 0in
Weight: 18 tons
Cylinders: 15in×20in
Pressure: 120lb

The first engine to be built at the newly opened Crewe Works of the Grand Junction Railway in 1845. No 49 *Columbine* was the first of a long series of locomotives designed by Alexander Allan, the particular feature of which was the combined outside cylinders and smokebox, these together forming a most graceful series of curves at the front end of the locomotives, and a distinctive type of framing with a deepened extension at the front end to support the slide bars carrying the crosshead for the pistons. No 49 was re-numbered in the duplicate list as No 1868 in 1872, and was transferred to the Engineer's Department in 1877 as *Engineer Bangor*, being replaced on that duty in 1902 by a 2–4–0. Thereafter it was preserved in the paint shop at Crewe, and now at the National Railway Museum, York.

S&DR 0–6–0 No 25 'Derwent' 1845

Driving wheels: 4ft 0in
Weight: 22 tons
Cylinders: 14½in×24in
Pressure: 75lb

Built by W. & A. Kitching, of Darlington in 1845 to the design of Timothy Hackworth, for the Stockton & Darlington Railway; one of several engines of the class, the last of which was turned out in 1848. It was later purchased by Messrs Pease & Partners, Darlington, for use on their private lines, and was eventually presented by them to the North Eastern Railway in 1898 for preservation. It is housed in the museum at Darlington North Road station.

The shell of another very similar engine *Bradyll*, built in 1835, was on withdrawal in 1875 improvised as a snow plough at Hetton Colliery, in which form it remained until the late 1940s. It is now preserved in this condition. It consists only of wheels, frames and boiler. The illustration shows *Derwent* on display at Darlington station in 1964.

Furness Railway 0–4–0 No 3 'Coppernob'   1846

Driving wheels: 4ft 9in
Weight: 19½ tons
Cylinders: 14in×24in
Pressure: 110lb
Tractive effort: 7,718lb

This engine is a good example of Bury's 0–4–0 tender engines with bar frames. On the Furness Railway the type continued to be built up to 1861 by W. Fairbairn & Son, who perpetuated the design after the original firm of Bury Curtis & Kennedy had ceased production. No 3 *Coppernob*, so nicknamed be-

cause of its bright dome-shaped copper firebox, was built in 1846 and remained at work together with a sister engine No 4, until 1900. At that time they were the oldest engines still in service in the country. No 3 was installed in a large glass housing outside the station at Barrow in Furness, and remained there, except for a visit to Wembley Exhibition in 1924/5, until World War II, when the glass case was damaged by enemy action. After storage at Horwich Works, then exhibition at Clapham, it is now in the National Railway Museum.

LNWR 2–2–2 No 3020 'Cornwall'   1847

Driving wheels: 8ft 6in
Cylinders: 17½in×24in
Pressure: 140lb
Tractive effort: 8,575lb

Built by Francis Trevithick at Crewe in 1847, this famous engine originally had the boiler beneath the driving axle, to obtain a low centre of gravity. This was possible only because of the very large diameter of the driving wheels. Originally constructed as a 2–2–2, it

was very soon altered to a 4–2–2. It was completely rebuilt by John Ramsbottom in 1858, reverting to a 2–2–2, with the boiler in the orthodox position; it has been very little altered since. Originally No 173 it was placed on the duplicate list as No 3020 in 1886. It ran in ordinary service until 1902, when it was withdrawn and laid aside. In 1907 it was put to work again, attached to a special saloon for the use of the Company's directors. This was a six-wheeled vehicle with a small coal

No 186 had been rebuilt in 1937 with Belpaire firebox and superheater, but another of the same class, No 184 built at Inchicore in 1880, and which never received a Belpaire boiler, superheater or extended smokebox, was retained by the CIE and presented to the RPSI in 1977, was restored to running condition for filming purposes in 1978, and will now work main line steam specials in Ireland.

South Devon Railway 0–4–0 'Tiny' 1868

Driving wheels : 3ft 0in
Cylinders: 9in × 12in

This curious little broad gauge (7ft 0¼in) vertical boiler engine was built by Sara & Co, Plymouth in 1868 for the South Devon Railway. On being taken over by the GWR it became No 1280 in its list, and on withdrawal in 1883 was put to work as a stationary boiler in Newton Abbot shops. It was finally retired in 1927, since when it has stood on a plinth at Newton Abbot station.

Now at Buckfastleigh.

NER 2–2–4T No 66 'Aerolite' 1869

Driving wheels : 5ft 8in
Weight: 44½ tons
Cylinders: (1) 13in × 20in
(1) 18½in × 20in
Pressure: 175lb

A very much rebuilt engine, it was originally a 2–2–2WT with outside frames built by Fletcher in 1869. In 1892 it was rebuilt by William Worsdell as a Von Borries two-cylinder compound, a leading bogie being added, making it a 4–2–2T. It was a very handsome engine in this form. Its final metamorphosis took place in 1902, when it became a 2–2–4T, and its original name *Aerolite* was restored. It ran thus until 1933, usually being employed on hauling an official's saloon.

Restored to NER livery, it now rests in the National Railways Museum, York.

22

engine of the class, No 156A (later No 1), was also similarly preserved in 1930, but after only two years was broken up. Fortunately the second effort at retaining one of these interesting and long-lived engines met with more success, as a result of the efforts of the author and the Stephenson Locomotive Society.

GS&WR McDonnell 0–6–0 1866

Driving wheels: 5ft 2in
Weight: 43 tons
Cylinders: 18in×24in
Pressure: 160lb
Tractive effort: 17,170lb
Gauge: 5ft 3in

Built by Sharp Stewart & Co in 1866, this particular engine was one of a long series (by Irish standards) turned out between 1866 and 1903, a total of 111 being eventually completed, the most numerous class ever to be seen in Ireland. They were built to the design of Alexander McDonnell, who later went to the North Eastern Railway. A general purpose mixed traffic design, they were to be seen all over the system and on all kinds of work right to the end of the steam era. It is now the property of the Railway Preservation Society of Ireland, Whitehead, Co Antrim, and periodically works steam rail tours, both in Northern and Southern Ireland.

obtained. Both engines were constructed by Fletcher Jennings in 1865, (works Nos 42 and 63). Each of them was in turn latterly out of service for a few years, but both have been completely renewed and thus achieved a working life of over a century.

The illustrations show Nos 1 and 2 at Towyn.

No 2 *Dolgoch* 0–4–0WT
Driving wheels: 2ft 3in
Weight: 8½ tons
Cylinders: 8in × 15in
Pressure: 70lb

LNWR 0–4–0T 'Pet'   1865

Driving wheels : 1ft 4in
Cylinders: 5½in × 6in
Gauge: 1ft 6in

One of a series of seven locomotives used for shunting over the 18in gauge system in Crewe works, *Pet* was built in 1865. The railway, which was used for transporting boilers and other heavy parts of machinery around the works, was abandoned in 1929 and the locomotives scrapped with the exception of *Pet*, which was preserved in the paint shop. It is now housed in the Talyllyn Narrow Gauge Museum at Towyn.

MR 2–4–0 No 158A   1866

Driving wheels : 6ft 3in
Weight: (engine) 41¼ tons
Cylinders: 18in × 24in
Pressure: 140lb
Tractive effort: 12,338lb

Built by W. Kirtley at Derby in 1866, MR No 158 one of a series of 29 engines. It became

158A in 1896, No 2 in 1907, LMS No 2 in 1923, and No 20002 in 1934. Withdrawn from service 1947 and repainted in MR style (pre-1907). Kept in Derby works for many years and periodically brought out on special occasions for exhibition, it is now on the Midland Railway Trust's preservation premises at Butterley. It is interesting to note that another

LNWR 0–4–0ST No 1439

Driving wheels: 4ft 0in
Weight: 22¾ tons
Cylinders: 14in×20in
Pressure: 120lb

Designed by John Ramsbottom and built at Crewe in 1865. Placed on duplicate list in 1885 and sold to Kynochs in 1919. Presented by Imperial Chemical Industries (Kynoch's successors) in 1954 to the British Transport Commission for preservation. Repainted in old LNWR green livery with the original number 1439. Now in Staffordshire County Council Industrial Museum at Shugborough Hall.

Talyllyn Railway 0–4–2ST and 0–4–0WT 'Talyllyn' and 'Dolgoch'

No 1 *Talyllyn* 0–4–2ST
Driving wheels: 2ft 3in
Weight: 8½ tons
Cylinders: 8in×16in
Pressure: 70lb
Gauge: 2ft 3in

The two original engines of the Talyllyn Railway, which worked the line during the whole of its existence, until 1951, when it was threatened with closure, but taken over by the Talyllyn Railway Preservation Society, since when some additional engines have been

Driving wheels: 2ft 0in
Weight: 8½ tons
Cylinders: 8¼in × 12in
Pressure: 140lb
Gauge: 1ft 11½in

Four surviving engines out of six built by George England & Co between 1863 and 1867. All originally had side tanks, which were later replaced by the present saddle, and ran with small four-wheeled tenders, making them in effect both tank and tender engines. This was the first attempt to use steam locomotives on such a narrow gauge, and was at the instigation of Charles Spooner, Festiniog General Manager and Engineer. Previously the railway had been worked by horse traction. It was closed in 1946, but fortunately reopened by the Festiniog Railway Society in 1955. No 2 *Prince* (illustrated) was the first engine to be restored to traffic; its sister No 1 *Princess* is now on exhibition at Blaenau Ffestiniog.

The remains of No 5 *Welsh Pony* are still in existence although probably beyond the likelihood of renovation, whilst No 4 *Palmerston* has been purchased by Group Five Engine Association and is at Draycott in the Clay, Staffordshire.

Metropolitan Railway 4—4—0T No 23   1864

Driving wheels: 5ft 10in
Weight: 45 tons
Cylinders: 17in × 26in
Pressure: 160lb
Tractive effort: 13,056lb

One of the last survivors of the original 66 Beyer Peacock 4—4—0Ts built from 1864 onwards for working the Metropolitan Railway. Most of them were scrapped or sold when the Inner Circle was electrified in 1905, but a few were retained for departmental duties, and also for working the Brill branch. No 23 was built by Beyer Peacock in 1866 (works No 710), and passed to the London Passenger Transport Board in 1934. It was renumbered L45 in 1938, and remained in service throughout the war. After withdrawal it was retained at Neasden, and has since been repainted in Metropolitan livery and restored to its early condition. It is now in the new London Transport Museum at Covent Garden.

Part Two

Furness Railway 0–4–0ST   1863

Driving wheels: No 7 4ft 10in; No 17 4ft 3in
Other particulars not available

Two 0–4–0STs built by Sharp Stewart & Co in 1863 and 1865 (works Nos 1435 and 1585) for the Furness Railway, No 18 and No 25. Sold in 1870 and 1873 respectively to Barrow Steelworks, becoming Nos 7 and 17 in that company's list. Both worked until 1960, when they were withdrawn from service and placed on public exhibition. No 7, now named *Chloe*, is at the Hastwell Training Centre, Abbey Road, Barrow, and No 17 at the Stone Cross Special School, Ulverston. The illustration shows No 7 at work at Barrow Steelworks in 1953.

Festiniog Railway 0–4–0ST   1863

Padarn Railway 0–4–0 'Fire Queen'   1848

Driving wheels: 4ft 6in
Cylinders: 13in × 22in
Pressure: 60lb
Wheelbase: 12ft

One of two locomotives built in 1848 by Horlock of Northfleet Ironworks for the 4ft 0in gauge 'main line' of the Dinorwic Slate Co,

Jenny Lind and *Fire Queen.* Both were taken out of service in 1886.

Fire Queen was preserved sealed up in its shed, at the Company's headquarters at Llanberis until December 1969 when it was moved to the National Trust Museum at Penrhyn Castle, Bangor, Gwynedd.

Wantage Tramway 0–4–0WT No 5 'Shannon'   1857

Driving wheels: 3ft 0in
Weight: 15 tons
Cylinders: 9in × 12in
Pressure: 120lb

Built by George England & Co of Hatcham Ironworks, for the Sandy & Potton Railway. Later it came into the hands of the LNWR. It was tried out for a short time on the Cromford & High Peak Railway, but was disposed of in 1878 to the Wantage Tramway. This line was closed in 1945, when the engine was removed to Swindon Works, and in the following year the GWR repainted it for preservation. On the LNWR it had been No 1863, becoming No 5 on the Wantage. Originally it had been named *Shannon*, although not under LNWR or WTR ownership. It was, however, fitted with new nameplates when restored. Its first resting place was under an awning on the platform at Wantage Road station, closed in 1964, since when it has been moved to the Didcot Railway Centre where it is occasionally steamed. It took part in the 150th Anniversary procession at Shildon in August 1975.

bunker next to the engine, later replaced by an ordinary tender, and used with a moderate separate bogie saloon. It remained on these duties until 1927 when it was finally retired and kept in Crewe paint shop. It was latterly in Clapham museum, but since that installa-

tion's closure it has been returned to Crewe. The illustration shows the engine in its final form. It has recently been on loan to the Severn Valley Railway for restoration to working order.

GS&WR Bury 2–2–2 No 36

1848

Driving wheels: 6ft 0in
Weight: 22 tons 19 cwt
Cylinders: 15in × 20in
Pressure: 80lb
Gauge: 5ft 3in

A second example of the Bury type of locomotive much in use in the 1840s. No 36 was delivered to the GS&WR in 1848, the last of 14 engines of the class, and was the last to run in 1874. It was then kept at Inchicore, and

mounted on a pedestal in front of the office there in 1903. The copper firebox was removed for scrap during World War I. It was exhibited at the Darlington Centenary Exhibition in 1925, and on return to Ireland was dumped in the yard at Inchicore. Fortunately O. V. Bulleid of the Southern Railway, on his appointment as Chief Mechanical Engineer of the CIE, had the engine restored in 1950, and it now rests at Cork station, as illustrated.

GNR 4–2–2 No 1

1870

Driving wheels : 8ft 0in
Weight: 38 tons 9 cwt
Cylinders: 18in × 28in
Pressure: 140lb

One of the best known of all historic locomotives, Patrick Stirling's No 1 of 1870 even gained the distinction of appearing on a postage stamp, although regrettably not in this country, but strangely enough in Uruguay. The first of a remarkable series of locomotives which did fine work over the GNR main line for many years, it was withdrawn in 1907, placed in honourable retirement and eventually found a permanent resting place in York Museum. In 1938 it was steamed again and worked a few special trains, notably one organised by the Railway Correspondence & Travel Society (the first of all privately-organised rail tours, which have become such a feature of recent years), since when it has once again been resident at York, and can still be seen. It took part in the 1975 150th Anniversary procession, although not in steam. It is now housed in the National Railway Museum.

LBSCR Stroudley Classes A1, A1X 0–6–0T

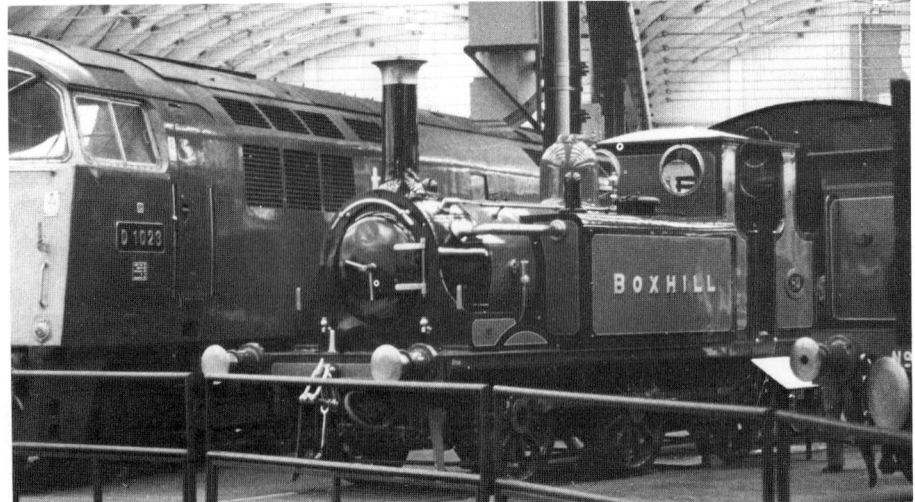

Driving wheels: 4ft
Weight: 27½ tons
Cylinders: 12in×20in
14in×20in (AIX)
Pressure: 150lb
Tractive effort: 7,650lb
10,695lb (AIX)

One of the most preserved classes, as these attractive engines were particularly long lived, the design having been introduced by William Stroudley in 1872. By the time the last survivor was withdrawn in 1963 there was a considerable demand for such historic locomotives. No 82 *Boxhill,* built in 1880, was works locomotive shunter at Brighton for many years (under the number 380S). On withdrawal in 1946 was restored to its original livery. Now officially preserved by BR, it stood in Clapham Museum until the latter's closure in 1973. It is in original Class A1 condition, whereas the other survivors (except No 54) are all rebuilt with extended smokeboxes as Class A1X. *Boxhill* is now in the National Railway Museum at York. Another of the class had been sold to the SE&CR in 1904,

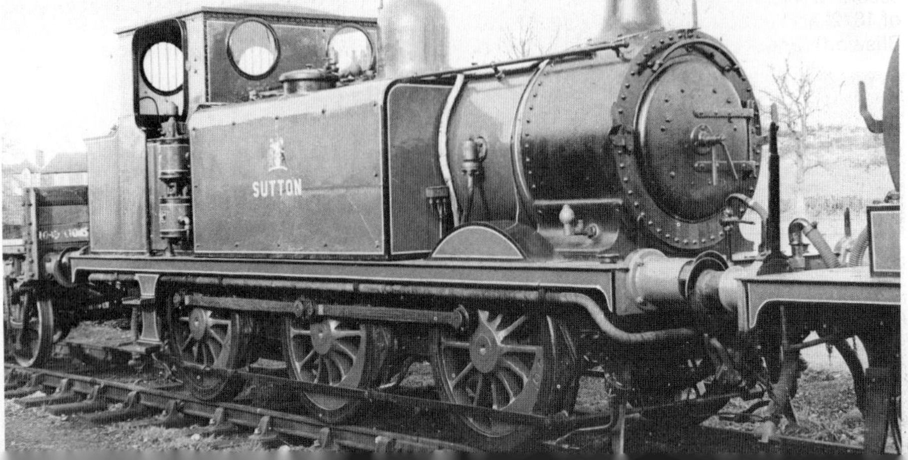

worked for many years and are never likely to again. After temporary closure, the railway was reopened in 1967. By 1974 however only the Port Erin branch was still in use, and this section is now kept open to Douglas as a tourist attraction operated by the Government as the Isle of Man Railways. Engines latterly in use were Nos 4 *Loch,* 10 *G. H. Wood,* 11 *Maitland,* 12 *Hutchinson* and 13 *Kissack.* No 9 *Douglas* may also be restored to working order. Nos 1 *Sutherland* and 16 *Mannin* are preserved in the Isle of Man Museum, Port

Erin. No 14 *Thornhill* is privately preserved at Ramsey. No 3 *Pender* has been transferred to the mainland for display in the North West Museum of Science and Industry, Manchester. No 6 *Peveril* is with the National Railway Museum's collection.

LSWR 2–4–0WT

1874

Driving wheels : 5ft 7in
Weight: 37 tons 16 cwt
Cylinders: 16½in×20in
Pressure: 60lb
Tractive effort: 11,050lb

Introduced by W. G. Beattie in 1874 for suburban working, three of this class were retained for many years (about three times as long as the life of most of their sisters) for working the lightly laid Wenford Bridge mineral branch in

Cornwall. Much rebuilt and renewed during that time, Nos 30585, 30586 and 30587 finally succumbed in December 1962 in favour of small GWR 0–6–0PTs only to be replaced in turn after a short time by diesels. Two of the three survivors are preserved, No 30585 being part of the National Railway Museum collection, and currently on loan to the Dart Valley Railway at Buckfastleigh. No 30587 has been restored to working order as No E0314 at Quainton Road.

S&DR 0–6–0 No 1275

1874

Driving wheels : 5ft 1in
Weight: 35 tons
Cylinders: 17in×26in
Pressure: 130lb

Bouch's 1001 class 0–6–0 freight engine for the Stockton & Darlington Railway, was developed from Stephenson's original 'long-boiler' design. No 1275 was built by Dübs &

Co in 1874, and lasted long enough to be absorbed by the LNER at the Grouping. It took part in the 1925 Darlington Centenary Exhibition, afterwards being restored to NER livery and placed in York Museum. It has now been transferred to the museum at North Road station, Darlington.

MR 0–6–0T No 1708   1874

Driving wheels: 4ft 7in
Weight: 39 tons 11 cwt
Cylinders: 17in×24in
Pressure: 50lb
Tractive effort: 16,080lb

One of a series of 280 0–6–0Ts built by S. W. Johnson between 1874 and 1900. Originally No 1418, this particular locomotive was one of a batch constructed at Derby in 1880. It became No 1708 in 1907, LMS 1708 in 1923. BR Nos M1708 in 1948, and 41708 in 1949.

Withdrawn from stock at the end of 1966, No 41708 at that time was the oldest engine on British Railways. It had been rebuilt with Belpaire firebox in 1926, but in common with many others of its class retained the 'half cab'. Illustration shows the engine as finally running in 1965. It is now the property of the 1708 Locomotive Preservation Trust Ltd. After several years on the K&WVR, it is now with the Midland Railway Trust at Butterley, after a period in store near Dunstable.

LBSCR Stroudley Class E1 0–6–0T No 110   1874

Driving wheels : 4ft 6in
Weight: 44 tons 3 cwt
Cylinders: 17in × 24in
Pressure: 170lb
Tractive effort: 18,600lb

One of William Stroudley's E1 Class introduced in 1874. No 110 *Burgundy* was built at
Brighton in 1877. In 1927 it was sold to the
Cannock and Rugeley Collieries, Hednesford,
on which line it became No 9 *Cannock Wood*,
subsequently coming into the possession of
the National Coal Board. It was preserved by
the Railway Preservation Society, at Chasewater, Staffordshire, but has now gone to the
East Somerset Railway as BR No 32110.

NER Fletcher 2–4–0 No 910   1875

Driving wheels : 7ft 0in
Weight: 39 tons 1 cwt
Cylinders: 17in × 24in
Pressure: 140lb

One of Mr Fletcher's celebrated 2–4–0
express engines, built at Gateshead in 1875.
Became LNER No 910 (Class E6), withdrawn
in 1925; restored to NER livery and placed in
the original York Museum. It took part in the
1975 150th Anniversary procession at
Shildon. It is now part of the permanent collection of the National Railway Museum at
York.

GS&WR 0–6–0T No 90

Driving wheels : 3ft 8½in
Weight: 22 tons 9 cwt
Cylinders: 12in × 18in
Pressure: 50lb
Tractive effort: 7,425lb
Gauge: 5ft 3in

Built in 1875 as an 0–6–4T combined engine and coach for the Castleisland Railway. It be- came GS&WR No 90 in 1879. The carriage portion was removed in 1915 and it became a small 0–6–0T, for which it was suited for various light duties, among them for working over the Timoleague & Courtmacsherry Rail- way. It last worked at Cork in 1961, when it was restored for preservation, being on exhibition at Mallow.

L&YR Barton Wright 0–6–0 No 957

Driving wheels : 4ft 6in
Weight: 39 tons 1 cwt
Cylinders: 17½in × 26in
Pressure: 140lb
Tractive effort: 17,545lb

Of the same origin as No 11456, this was one of the same class which remained as originally built as a tender engine. No 957 was

built by Beyer Peacock & Co in 1887 (works No 2840), became LMS No 12044 at the Grouping, and eventually BR No 52044. Withdrawn from service in 1959, it was acquired privately for preservation and repainted in L&YR colours. Now to be seen at Haworth, headquarters of the Keighley & Worth Valley Railway restored to BR black livery.

GER 0–4–0ST No 229   1876

Driving wheels : 3ft 7in
Weight: 24 tons 4 cwt
Cylinders: 12in × 20in
Pressure: 140lb
Tractive effort: 7,970lb

Built by Neilson & Co in 1876 (works No 2119).

One of a series of eight engines built between 1874 and 1903 as Nos 209, 210 and 226 to 231. No 29 became 0229 in 1914 and shortly afterwards was sold out of service to the Admiralty. It became the property of the Fairfield Shipbuilding Co of Chepstow in 1917 and has been out of use for several years.

Corris Railway No 3 'Sir Haydn'   1878

Driving wheels : 2ft 6in
Weight: 23 tons 16 cwt
Cylinders: 7in × 12in
Pressure: 140
Gauge: 2ft 3in

Built by the Falcon Engineering Works in 1878 (works No 323). The Corris Railway was taken over by the GWR in 1930, and in turn by BR in

1948, in which year the line was closed. This engine however, with one other, was acquired in 1951 by the Talyllyn Railway on which line it now runs as No 3 *Sir Haydn*. It is interesting to note that it has carried the same No 3 under its four different ownerships. The illustration shows the engine at Towyn in 1974.

Festiniog Railway Fairlie 0–4–4–0T   1879

Driving wheels : 2ft 9¼in
Weight: 24 tons*
Cylinders: (4) 9in × 14in
Pressure: 160lb
Tractive effort: 6,059lb*
Gauge: 1ft 11½in

Robert Fairlie's design of 1870 to provide a more powerful engine than the 0–4–0STs, (qv) in order to handle more lengthy trains, to avoid the costly necessity of doubling the line. Fairlie's solution was a locomotive incorporating two separate boilers with a common

central firebox separated into two portions, one for each boiler, and each with its independent firehole door. Two independent swivelling steam bogies have steam connections through flexible pipes, the driver occupies one side of the central cab, and the fireman the other, on which the firebox is situated.

The first Fairlie engine had been built in 1852, for the Semmering Incline in Austria, but it was its application to so narrow a gauge on the Festiniog which attracted railway engineers from many parts of the world, and the patented idea was subsequently used in Sweden, Russia, and other countries.

Of the four engines built for the Festiniog two survive, No 10 *Merddyn Emrys,* and what was originally No 11 *Livingston Thompson,* built at the Company's own works at Boston Lodge in 1879 and 1885 respectively. The latter engine was later renumbered 3, and renamed *Taliesin* in 1932. In 1962 it became *Earl of Merioneth* with the name in English on one side, and in Welsh *Iarll Meironwydd* on the other. It is at present awaiting restoration as *Livingston Thompson* for display. It was working until 1971, and parts of it were used in the construction of a new locomotive, *Earl of Merioneth.*

*The new *Earl of Merioneth* has a weight of 31 tons and a tractive effort of 9,277lb.

Gwendraeth Valleys Railway 0–6–0ST 'Margaret'

1878

Driving wheels : 4ft 0in
Weight: 31 tons
Cylinders: 16¼in × 24in
Pressure: 140lb

The small Gwendraeth Valleys Railway (not to be confused with the Burry Port & Gwendraeth Valley, see page 59) was a subsidiary of the Kidwelly Tinplate works. *Margaret,* which was purchased from the GWR in 1910, had been built in 1878 by Fox Walker & Co for the North Pembrokeshire & Fishguard Railway and was taken over by the Great Western in 1898 as No 1378. It duly became Gwendraeth Valleys No 2, but although this concern was also taken over by the Great Western in 1923, the engine became the property of the Kidwelly Tinplate Co, for

whom it continued in service until 1941, when the works were closed. The contractors who took over the works for dismantling, Messrs Zammit of Llanelly, for some reason allowed the engine to hibernate in its shed, where rather extraordinarily it remained until quite recently, apparently forgotten, and unknown except to locomotive historians. It is now officially preserved at Scolton Manor County Park Museum, Pembroke.

LNWR Webb 0–6–2T No 1054 1881

Driving wheels: 4ft 3in
Weight: 43¾ tons
Cylinders: 17in×24in
Pressure: 150lb
Tractive effort: 16,530lb

F. W. Webb's outstanding engine for performing so many of the less spectacular duties in running a great railway; 300 of them were built at Crewe between 1881 and 1896, this particular engine in 1888. No 1054 became LMS No 7799 at the Grouping, it was in fact officially withdrawn from service in 1939,

but for the incidence of war would never have survived to become the lasting monument it now has. It became BR No 58926 at Nationalisation, and spent its last years at Abergavenny working over the mountainous line to Merthyr. Its final duty was to work the last train, a special organised by the Stephenson Locomotive Society, to Merthyr on 5 January 1958, after which the line was completely closed. It was at first preserved at Penrhyn Castle Museum, Bangor, but in 1973 was removed to Dinting Railway Centre.

LBSCR 0–4–2 No 214 'Gladstone' 1882

Driving wheels : 6ft 6in
Weight: 38 tons 14 cwt
Cylinders: 18¼in×26in
Pressure: 150lb

The first engine to be preserved privately, a project undertaken by the Stephenson Loco-

motive Society, largely through the efforts of the late J. N. Maskelyne. The first of William Stroudley's well known front-coupled express engines, built at Brighton in 1882, No 214 *Gladstone* ran until 1927, when it was withdrawn from service and restored to its original state. It had been rebuilt with a modi-

33

fied boiler and lost its distinctive copper capped chimney, and had also become No 618 in 1920 (SR No B618 at the Grouping). Lack of accommodation proved a major problem at the time, but eventually the LNER agreed to house it in the original museum at York.

The photograph shows the engine at the National Railway Museum, York in 1977.

LSWR Adams 4–4–2T No 488   1882

Driving wheels : 5ft 7in
Weight: 55 tons 3 cwt
Cylinders: 17½in × 24in
Pressure: 160lb
Tractive effort: 14,920lb

By 1929 only two of the 71-strong class remained, to work the Lyme Regis branch over which, with its severe curves, no other engines were suitable. They were joined in 1946 by this engine which was built in 1885 by Neilson & Co (works No 3209), as LSWR No 488, and placed on the duplicate list as No 0488 in 1914. Sold in 1917 to Ridham Salvage Depot, Sittingbourne who sold it to the East Kent Light Rly as No 5, in 1919. Returning to the SR in 1946 it took its rightful number 3488. It duly became BR No 30583. Withdrawn in 1961, No 30583 was acquired by the Bluebell Railway, where it now works repainted in LSWR Drummond livery, as No 488.

B&NCR 0–4–0T tram locomotive

1882

Driving wheels : 2ft 4½in
Weight: 8 tons (approx.)
Cylinders: 8in × 12in

Two of Kitson's typical tram engines of the period, built in 1882 and 1883 (works Nos T56 and T84) for the Belfast & Northern Counties Railway, for working its roadside tramway from Portrush to Portstewart. They passed into the ownership of the Midland Railway of England when that line took over the B&NCR, in 1903. The line closed in 1926 and the two engines were placed in store at Belfast. Both are now preserved in museums, No 1 in Hull Museum and No 2, restored to B&NCR

colours, in Belfast Museum. The illustration shows the engines in store at Belfast in 1930.

GWR Dean 0–6–0 No 2516

1883

Driving wheels : 5ft 2in
Weight: 36 tons 16 cwt
Cylinders: 17½in × 24in
Pressure: 180lb
Tractive effort: 18,140lb

William Dean's design of 1883, although intended primarily as a freight engine, did much passenger work. In all 260 of them were built, and many served overseas during both world wars. No 2516, the engine which has been preserved, was built at Swindon in 1897. It received a Belpaire firebox in 1913, and was superheated in 1935. Withdrawn from service in 1956, it is now in Swindon Museum.

GER Class J15 0–6–0 No 564

1883

Driving wheels: 4ft 11in
Weight: 37 tons 2 cwt
Cylinders: 17½in × 24in
Pressure: 160lb
Tractive effort: 16,940lb

The GER's 'maid of all work' locomotives, 189 of which were built between 1883 and 1913. Once to be seen anywhere in the eastern counties on all kinds of duties from express passenger to local pick-up goods, the last of them were withdrawn from service in 1962. Four were retained for a time with a view to one of them being preserved by the then Midland & Great Northern Joint Preservation Society, the engine finally selected being No 65462 (originally GER No 564). It has now been restored to working order and GER livery, with its original number, and can be seen on the North Norfolk Railway.

Cavan & Leitrim Railway 4–4–0T No 2

1884

Beyer Peacock tram locomotive 'John Bull'   1885

Driving wheels : 2ft 6in
Weight: 16 tons
Cylinders: 9½in × 12in
Pressure: 150lb

Built by Beyer Peacock (works No 2464) to the order of the New South Wales Govt, this engine was shipped to Australia in April 1885. When used on the Sydney Tramways, it was found to be too heavy on fuel, and was transferred to the Wellagong-Clifton section of the NSWGR until that line was connected with the South Coast main line. It then 'disappeared' and nothing more was heard until it re-appeared in Manchester in 1890 at Beyer Peacock's works as its shunting locomotive No 2, in which capacity it remained in active service until 1959. It was acquired by the Tramway Museum Society, Crich, in May 1962, to be its only steam locomotive. In full working order, it is sometimes used in pas-

senger service, usually in conjunction with an 1873 trailer from Oporto, Portugal, as seen above.

CR 4–2–2 No 123   1886

Driving wheels: 7ft
Cylinders: 18in × 26in
Pressure: 150lb
Tractive effort: 12,785lb

Built in 1886 by Neilson & Co, this was the only engine of its class, and the only 4–2–2 to run on a Scottish Railway. No 123 took a prominent part in the 1888 race to the north. Renumbered 1123 by the CR in 1914, she be-

came LMS No 14010 at the Grouping. Withdrawn in 1935, by then the last single wheeled express engine in service in the country, she was laid aside for preservation, and repainted in CR blue livery. In 1958 she was given a complete overhaul and put back into working order to haul enthusiasts specials, which she did for a number of years. She now rests permanently in Glasgow Transport Museum.

NER Class J21 0–6–0 No 876 · 1886

Driving wheels: 5ft 1¼in
Weight: 43¾ tons
Cylinders: 19in × 24in
Pressure: 160lb
Tractive effort: 19,240lb

A class of 201 engines built between 1886 and 1894, most of them as 2-cylinder compounds but 30 were turned out as simples. All the compounds were converted to simple propulsion from 1900 onwards. This particular engine came out from Gateshead in 1889 as NER No 876 (works No 8 of 1889). Latterly it

had received a superheater and piston valves. It was withdrawn from service in November 1939, but subsequently reinstated and continued in service until 1962. It was renumbered 5033 in 1946 under the LNER renumbering scheme and eventually BR No 65033. It lay in Darlington yard for several years after withdrawal in a deteriorating condition. Until recently its fate seemed in much doubt, although it had been envisaged that it would be preserved. It is now at the Beamish Museum, County Durham, and has been restored to working order as NER No 876.

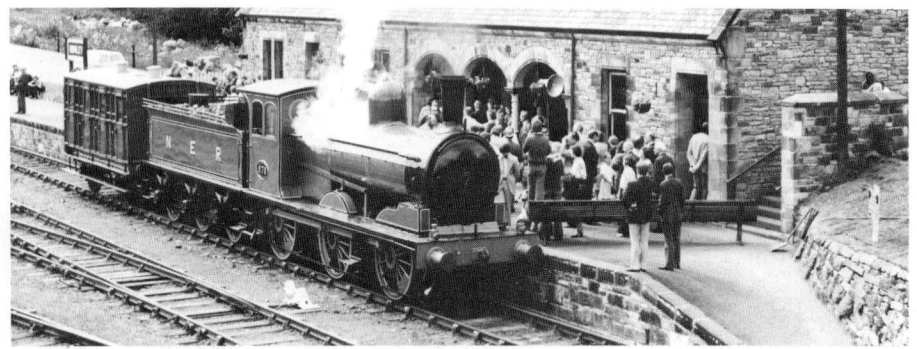

NLR 0–6–0T No 2650 · 1887

Driving wheels: 4ft 4in
Weight: 45½ tons
Cylinders: 17in × 24in
Pressure: 160lb
Tractive effort: 18,140lb

Built in 1887 for the North London Railway, and was originally No 116. Taken over by the

LNWR in 1909 and then became No 2650 in that company's list. It became LMS No 7505 in 1926, No 27505 in 1934, and finally BR No 58850. Withdrawn from service in 1960 (the last NLR engine in existence) and acquired by the Bluebell Railway. It was restored to LNWR condition as 2650, but awaits overhaul at present.

Driving wheels : 3ft 6in
Weight: 26 tons
Cylinders: 14in×20in
Pressure: 150lb
Tractive effort: 1,190lb
Gauge: 3ft 0in

Built by Stephenson & Co in 1884 for the Cavan & Leitrim Railway. It bore the name

Kathleen until 1947, and latterly was known as CIE No 2L. It ran until the line closed in 1959, has since been repainted and is now to be seen in Belfast Museum. Another of the class No 3 *Lady Edith* has gone to the USA together with a 2–6–2T from the Tralee and Dingle Railway, No 5. They are now at Pine Creek Railroad, New Jersey, both in working order.

Mersey Railway 0–6–4T 'Cecil Raikes' No 5   1885

Driving wheels : 4ft 7in
Weight: 67 tons 17 cwt
Cylinders: 21in×26in

One of a class of nine engines built by Beyer Peacock & Co in 1885 for working the trains through the tunnel of the Mersey Railway between Liverpool and Birkenhead. With gradients of 1 in 27 and 1 in 30 very powerful engines were required, and these were among the largest of their day. The line was electrified in 1904 and the engines disposed of. Four went to Australia, and at least one of them was at work until quite recently. Two

others, of which *Cecil Raikes* was one, were purchased by the Shipley collieries, Nottinghamshire, and this engine remained in service until 1954 afterwards being stored at Derby. The illustration shows the engine in 1952. At the time of writing it is undergoing restoration at Steamport Transport Museum, Southport.

NER Tennant 2–4–0 No 1463   1885

Driving wheels : 7ft 1in
Weight: 42 tons 1 cwt
Cylinders: 18in×24in
Pressure: 140lb

An NER design of 1885 produced by a committee under the chairmanship of the General Manager, Henry Tennant, of which No 1463 was the first locomotive. It became LNER No

1463 (Class E5) at the Grouping, was withdrawn in 1927, then repainted in North Eastern colours and placed in the original York Museum. In 1975 it was transferred to North Road station Museum, Darlington.

MNR 0–6–0T No 4 'Caledonia'   1885

Driving wheels : 3ft 3in
Gauge: 3ft 0in

This engine was built by Dübs & Co in 1885 (works No 2178) as MNR No 4 *Caledonia*. It was absorbed into the Isle of Man Railway in 1904 as No 15 and was the only non-standard engine in their stock, all the others being Beyer Peacock 2–4–0Ts (qv). It was too heavy for general use, and saw little service except during the winter months, when it proved very useful for snow clearance. In 1968 it was restored to its old Manx Northern livery of dark red and is now preserved in Port Erin Museum.

becoming No 751 on that line. On re-absorption in the Southern Railway in 1923 it became shunter at Lancing Carrriage works as No 680S. Withdrawn from service in 1963 it was restored to original condition as No 54 *Waddon* and is now on exhibition in Montreal, at the Canadian Railroad Museum.

The remainder may be summarised as follows:

No 55 *Stepney* and No 72 *Fenchurch* are on the Bluebell Railway. These had latterly been BR Nos 32655 and 32636, the last mentioned having been the property of the Newhaven Harbour Co from 1913 to 1927.

No 32640 (originally No 40 *Brighton*), later sold to the Isle of Wight Central Railway as their No 11, is now back on the island at Haven Street, premises of the Wight Locomotive Society, repainted in IWCR colours.

No 32662, originally No 62 *Martello*, is at Bressingham Hall, Diss, Norfolk, repainted in Marsh umber livery as LBSC No 662.

No 32678, formerly *Knowle*, for several years preserved at Butlin's holiday camp, Minehead, is now with the West Somerset Railway at Williton.

No 32646 was another which had been sold by the old Brighton Company, this time to the LSWR, in 1903, on which line it became No 734. It was later resold to the Isle of Wight, this time to the Freshwater Yarmouth and Newport Railway, as their No 2. When the SR took over the island's lines, they gave it the name *Freshwater,* later renumbering it W8. British Railways brought it back to the mainland in 1949, giving it its rightful number in accordance with its correct position in the main locomotive list as No 32646. Finally withdrawn from service in 1963, it was restored to its original livery as No 46 *Newington* and reposed outside a hostelry on Hayling Island known as the 'Hayling Billy'. It was transferred back to the Isle of Wight during 1979 and is to be restored as No W8 *Freshwater.*

Another engine has been acquired by the Kent & East Sussex Preservation Association. This was the most interesting of all, being one of the two original engines of the class built in 1872, No 70 *Poplar.* It had been sold to the Rother Valley Railway (later the Kent & East Sussex) as their No 3 *Bodiam,* although it had latterly lost its name and came back into BR stock as No 32670, the number it would eventually have carried had it never been sold in the first place. Withdrawn in 1963, it was purchased by Mr Wheele and is back at Tenterden as K&ESR 3 *Bodiam.* Another of the class No 32650 (originally No 50 *Whitechapel*), is owned by the Sutton Borough Council but is at present on loan to the Tenterden Railway Co Ltd bearing the name *Sutton* and numbered 10 in their list.

Oxford & Aylesbury Tramroad 0–4–0WT   1872

Driving wheels : 3ft 0in (geared)
Cylinders: (1) 7¾in × 10in

Built by Aveling & Porter in 1872 (works No 807) for the original Oxford and Aylesbury Tramroad, later the Brill branch of the Metropolitan Railway.

There were two of these engines (the second being Aveling & Porter works No 846 of 1872) and both were eventually sold to the Blisworth and Stowe Brick & Tile Co, Nether Heyford, Northants. The second engine was scrapped when the brickworks was closed in 1940, but No 807 remained derelict for a number of years until rescued by London Transport and restored. It was kept at Neasden for a time, then in Clapham Museum, but is now in the London Transport Museum, Covent Garden.

The illustration show a typical Brill branch scene.

LNWR 2–4–0 No 790 'Hardwicke' 1873

Driving wheels : 6ft 9in
Weight: 35 tons 12 cwt
Cylinders: 17in × 24in
Pressure: 150lb
Tractive effort: 10,918lb

Mr. F. W. Webb's most outstanding passenger class, *Hardwicke* was built at Crewe in 1873, and of a numerous class known as the Precedents which in the event formed the mainstay for working LNWR main line passenger trains for many years. It took part in the 1895 race to Scotland, became LMS No 5031 at the Grouping, and was withdrawn in 1932, being repainted in LNWR livery. For many years stored at Crewe, it is now based in the National Railway Museum at York. It took part in the 150th Anniversary procession at Shildon in August 1975, and is occasionally steamed for use on enthusiast specials. The illustration shows it on such a working piloting compound No 1000 near Poppleton in April 1976.

IoMR 2–4–0T 1873

Driving wheels : 3ft 9in
Weight: 18¼ tons
Cylinders: 11in × 18in
Pressure: 160lb
Gauge: 3ft 0in

Beyer Peacock built in all 14 of these engines between 1873 and 1926 for the Isle of Man Railway and one for the Manx Northern (absorbed into the Isle of Man in 1904). Most are still in existence, although some have not

MR 4–2–2 No 118

Driving wheels: 7ft 9½in
Cylinders: 19in×26in
Pressure: 170lb
Tractive effort: 15,279lb

The last remaining example of S. W. Johnson's celebrated single-wheeler, or 'spinners' as they were sometimes called, of which 95 were built between 1887 and 1900. No 118 was turned out from Derby works in 1897. She became No 673 in 1907, and LMS No 673 in 1923. Withdrawn from service in 1928 and repainted in MR colours with her original number, but no longer in working order. The replica chimney of original design is in fact a wooden dummy. Kept in Derby works for many years the engine was periodically brought out on special occasions. It was moved from Derby to the Stoneygate Museum, Leicester but is now at the Midland Railway Co's premises at Butterley, and has been restored to working order and 1907 condition as MR No 673.

L&YR 0–4–0T 'Wren'

Driving wheels: 1ft 4¼in
Weight: 3 tons 11½ cwt
Cylinders: 5in×6in
Gauge: 1ft 6in

A similar 18in gauge system to that at Crewe already described, at the Horwich works of the Lancashire & Yorkshire Railway. Of the eight locomotives in use, *Wren* was one of the original three built in 1887. Latterly only a small portion of the system was retained, requiring the use of only one locomotive, the others being scrapped. *Wren* thus outdated her sisters by many years, and on withdrawal in 1962 was sent to Clapham Museum, but has now been removed to the National Railway Museum, York. She is painted in L&YR livery.

NBR 0–4–0ST No 42 1887

Driving wheels: 3ft 8in
Weight: 27 tons 16 cwt
Cylinders: 14in × 20in
Pressure: 130lb
Tractive effort: 9,845lb

Holmes' NBR class for dock work and light shunting, nicknamed 'Pugs'. Originally North British Railway No 42, built in 1887, later 894, then again numbered 1094, then successively LNER No 10094, 10104, 8095, and finally BR No 68095. Withdrawn in 1962, it was acquired privately by J. M. Morris, director of Helical Springs Ltd of Lytham, Lancs, and is now in Lytham Motive Power Museum restored as NBR No 42. The illustration shows the engine at Edinburgh in 1961.

NBR 0–6–0 No 673 'Maude' 1888

Driving wheels: 5ft 0in
Weight: 41 tons 19 cwt
Cylinders: 18¼in × 26in
Pressure: 165lb
Tractive effort: 19,690lb

Matthew Holmes' standard design of 0–6–0 for the NBR was introduced in 1888. No 673 was built by Neilson & Co in 1891. She became LNER No 9673 in 1923, renumbered 5243 in 1946 and finally BR No 65243 at

Nationalisation. Along with several others of the class, she served overseas during World War I, and on return was given the name *Maude* which she has retained ever since. Withdrawn in 1966 and secured by the Scottish Railway Preservation Society, she may be seen at their museum in Falkirk. The illustration shows the engine as restored to NBR livery and numbered 673.

NER 0–4–0T No 1310

1888

Driving wheels: 4ft 0in
Weight: 22 tons 14 cwt
Cylinders: 14in × 20in
Pressure: 160lb
Tractive effort: 11,640lb

A small 0–4–0T design of T. W. Worsdell made between 1888 and 1897. NER Class H, became LNER Class Y7 at the Grouping. No 1310 was built at Gateshead in 1891. Sold in 1931 to the Pelaw Main Collieries, it later became NCB No 64. Purchased by the Steam Power Trust in 1965 for use on the Middleton Railway, Leeds. It has been repainted in NER livery, as shown in the illustration. Another, slightly enlarged version, built in 1923 as LNER Class 985, becoming BR No 68088 was sold in 1952 to Kirkby Bentinck Colliery. It is now at the GCR Main Line Steam Trust, Loughborough.

L&YR Aspinall 0–6–0 No 1122

1889

Driving wheels: 5ft 1in
Weight: 42 tons 3 cwt
Cylinders: 18in × 26in
Pressure: 180lb
Tractive effort: 21,130lb

One of J. A. F. Aspinall's numerous class of 0–6–0s, No 1300 was built at Horwich in 1896. It became LMS No 12322 at the Grouping and subsequently BR No 52322. Withdrawn from service in 1960, it was acquired privately and restored to L&YR colours under the number of another engine of the class, No 1122, which had been built in 1891. This particular engine (late No 12140) had however been rebuilt with Belpaire firebox and extended smoke-

box, whereas No 12322 had remained virtually in its original condition. It is now at Steamtown, Carnforth, and is being restored to running condition.

L&YR 2–4–2T No 1008 1889

Driving wheels: 5ft 8in
Weight: 55 tons 19 cwt
Cylinders: 18in × 26in
Pressure: 160lb
Tractive effort: 16,484lb

The first of Aspinall's numerous and very efficient class of 2–4–2Ts which did yeoman work on all the L&YR system until well after the Grouping, not becoming finally extinct until 1961. No 1008 itself was built in 1889, the first engine to be turned out from the then

new works at Horwich. It became LMS No 10621 in 1923, and was tried out for a time in 1926 on the Midland suburban services from Kentish Town shed but soon returned to its native system. As BR No 50621 it remained in service until 1954, when it was laid aside and restored to L&YR livery in 1958. For a time on loan to the Standard Gauge Steam Trust, Tyseley, it is now housed in the National Railway Museum, York.

LSWR Adams 0–4–4T No W24

Driving wheels: 4ft 10in
Weight: 46 tons 18 cwt
Cylinders: 17½in×24in
Pressure: 160lb
Tractive effort: 17,235lb

Adams' design for branch and miscellaneous work; 60 engines built between 1889 and 1895 of which 23 finally found their way to the Isle of Wight and after the Grouping, becoming the standard class over there until the end of steam working on 31 December 1966. No 209 was built in 1891, being transferred to the Island in 1925 and renumbered as SR W24, later receiving the name *Calbourne*. Withdrawn in March 1967, one of the last two to remain in steam, it has been acquired for preservation by the Wight Locomotive Society and has been restored to SR malachite green livery. It is illustrated at Wootton.

GER Holden 0–6–0T No 87

Driving wheels: 4ft 0in
Weight: 42 tons 9 cwt
Cylinders: 16½in×22in
Pressure: 180lb
Tractive effort: 19,090lb

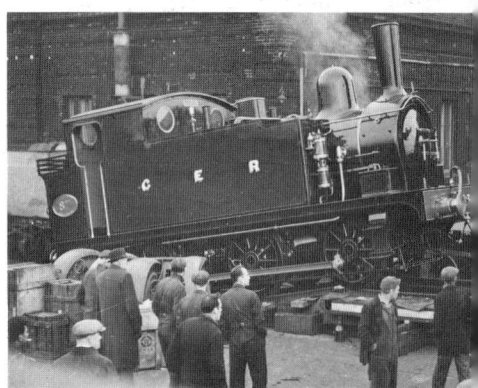

One of a numerous class introduced by J. Holden in 1890. Although primarily a shunting and local freight type, they also did much passenger work, particularly in the London suburban area and on country branches. No 87 was built at Stratford in 1904, it became LNER No 7087 at the Grouping, was renumbered 8633 in 1946, and finally BR No 68633 in 1948. Withdrawn from service in 1959 it was restored to GER condition. It was to be seen in Clapham Museum until the latter's closure in 1973, and has now been removed to the National Railway Museum, York.

City & South London Railway electric 0–4–0(Bo) 1890

Driving wheels: 2ft 3in
Weight: 12 tons
Horse power: 50
Pick-up: 3rd rail
Current: 500v dc
Tractive effort: 3,000lb

One of the first (not the original No 1, although it now bears this number) of the initial 14 engines built in 1890 by Mather and Platt for the newly opened City & South London Railway, London's first deep level tube. In all 52 engines were built, the last in 1901. The line was entirely re-constructed and extended between 1922 and 1926, going over to multiple-unit operation, all but two of the engines being scrapped. The older of these is now in the Science Museum. Another one, No 36 was preserved on a pedestal at Moorgate station, but was so badly damaged in an air raid during World War II that it had to be broken up. The engines were painted in the bright yellow livery of the LBSCR (Stroudley's 'improved engine green'). The engine is preserved in the Science Museum, South Kensington.

GER Holden 2–4–0 No 490 1891

Driving wheels: 5ft 8in
Weight: 40 tons 6 cwt
Cylinders: 17½in × 24in
Pressure: 160lb
Tractive effort: 14,700lb

A most useful and versatile mixed traffic class introduced by J. Holden in 1891, 100 examples being built. No 490 was turned out from Stratford in 1894, and became LNER No 7490 at the Grouping. Renumbered 7802 in 1942 and again 2785 in 1946. Finally as BR No 62785 it was withdrawn from service in 1959, restored to original GER condition. It is now displayed at the National Railway Museum, York.

L&YR 0–6–0ST No 752

Driving wheels: 4ft 6in
Weight: 43 tons 17 cwt
Cylinders: 17½in×26in
Pressure: 140lb
Tractive effort: 17,545lb

One of a numerous class of 0–6–0 engines designed by Barton Wright from 1876 onwards and subsequently reconstructed by Aspinall as saddle tanks from 1891 onwards (see page 30). No 752 was built by Beyer Peacock & Co in 1881 (works No 1989) and rebuilt as

0–6–0ST in 1896. Becoming LMS No 11456 it was sold in 1937 to the Coppull Colliery, Wigan. It was still at work in 1966 under the ownership of the National Coal Board, having been moved to Parsonage Colliery, Lancs, and by then being the only surviving engine of the class (the last example on BR having been withdrawn in 1964). It has been secured privately for preservation by the L&YR Saddletanks Fund, and is now on the Keighley & Worth Valley Railway restored to L&YR condition.

L&YR 0–4–0ST No 51218

Driving wheels: 3ft 0½in
Weight: 21¼ tons
Cylinders: 13in×18in
Pressure: 160lb
Tractive effort: 11,335lb

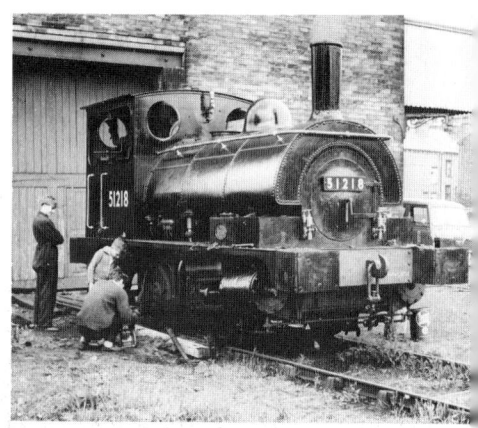

One of the class of L&YR dock shunters known as 'pugs' introduced by Aspinall in 1891. Originally L&YR No 68, built at Horwich in 1901, this engine became LMS No 11218 at the Grouping, and subsequently BR No 51218. Withdrawn from service in 1964. Another of the class, LMS No 1243 (L&YR No 19) which was sold in 1931 to Morris Mowlem, Contractors, and used in the Southampton Docks extension of the SR, has also like No 11218 been preserved by the L&Y Saddletanks Fund and both engines are now at the Haworth premises of the K&WVR. No 11243 has been restored to L&YR condition as No 19.

LSWR Adams 0–4–0T 1891

Driving wheels: 3ft 10in
Weight: 33 tons 9 cwt
Cylinders: 16in×22in
Pressure: 140lb
Tractive effort: 14,650lb

William Adams' design of small shunting engines introduced in 1891. Fourteen of them were allocated to Southampton Docks and given names. Two of these have been preserved. No 102, formerly *Granville* (name re-moved in 1950) was built at Nine Elms in 1893, and sold out of service in 1963. It was acquired by Sir Billy Butlin for exhibition at his holiday camp at Skegness, but is now at Bressingham Hall. Another of the class No 30096, sold to Corralls of Southampton and named *Corral Queen* has been purchased by the Bulleid Preservation Society. It is being restored as LSWR No 96 *Normandy* and is now on the Bluebell Railway. It is seen at Southampton in 1961.

West Clare 0–6–2T No 5 1892

Driving wheels: 3ft 6in
Weight: 35 tons 12 cwt
Cylinders: 15in × 20in
Pressure: 150lb
Tractive effort: 13,660lb
Gauge: 3ft 0in

Built by Dübs & Co in 1892 (works No 2890) and formerly named *Slieve Callan*, it became GSR No 5C in 1925, and was withdrawn from service in 1960 on closure of the line. It was restored to its old livery, and is now on public exhibition at Ennis, as depicted in the illustration.

LSWR Adams 4–4–0 No 563   1893

Driving wheels: 6ft 7in
Weight: 48 tons 11 cwt
Cylinders: 19in × 26in
Pressure: 175lb

The last surviving example of William Adams' final express engines for the LSWR, 60 of which were built (30 with 7ft 1in driving wheels). No 563 was turned out from Nine Elms in 1893, and ran until 1945, having been condemned in 1939 but later reinstated owing to the outbreak of World War II. It lay derelict at Eastleigh until 1948, when it was restored to its original condition, complete with stove pipe chimney, brass number plate, early livery and other details, and exhibited at Waterloo.

It was to be seen in Clapham Museum until the latter's closure in 1973, and is now displayed at the National Railway Museum, York.

NER 4–4–0 No 1621   1893

Driving wheels: 7ft 1in
Weight: 50 tons 2 cwt
Cylinders: 19in × 26in
Pressure: 160lb
Tractive effort: 15,001lb

Wilson Worsdell's 4–4–0 design of 1893, Class M (LNER Class D17/1) No 1621 was the second engine in the class, and distinguished

itself in the 1895 race to Scotland. It became LNER No 1621, and under the 1943 renumbering scheme (not actually put into effect until 1946) would have become No 2108, but it was withdrawn in 1945. It was then repainted in NER livery and placed in the old York Museum, being transferred to the new museum in 1975.

Shropshire & Montgomery Railway 0–4–2WT 'Gazelle'

1893

Driving wheels: 2ft 0in
Weight: 5½ tons
Cylinders: 4in×9in

Built by Dodman at King's Lynn in 1893 as a small 2–2–2WT inspection coach, later converted to an 0–4–2WT. Later acquired by the Shropshire and Montgomery Railway to become their No 1. Used in the 1920s for working the Criggion branch from Kinnerley Junction. This railway was acquired by the War Department during World War II, and after hostilities had ceased the engine was transferred to the Longmoor Military Railway, now disbanded. It has since been transferred to the National Railway Museum, York.

Highland Railway 4–6–0 No 103

1894

Driving wheels: 5ft 3in
Weight: (engine only) 56 tons
Cylinders: 20in×26in
Pressure: 175lb
Tractive effort: 24,555lb

Notable as being the first 4–6–0 tender engine in the British Isles. One of 15 built by Sharp Stewart & Co in 1894 to the designs of David Jones, No 103 became LMS No 17916 in 1923 and remained in service until 1934, when it was withdrawn and laid aside for preservation. It was duly restored in the old Highland Railway olive green, and kept at St Rollox works, where it remained until well after the war. In 1959 it was decided to put it in running order again to work special trains, and the smokebox wing plates, which had been removed under the LMS regime, were restored. It was also repainted in the short lived yellow livery, which had been introduced by William Stroudley (Stroudley's 'improved engine green'). Now preserved in Glasgow Transport Museum. Whether No 103 ever actually ran in this livery when first built is in fact in doubt

Duke of Sutherland's Railway 0–4–4T 'Dunrobin'

1895

This 0–4–4T was built by Sharp Stewart & Co in 1895 for the Duke of Sutherland's private railway between Golspie and Helmsdale, opened in 1871. The engine was kept in its own private shed at Dunrobin, but the Duke and his heirs had the right to run it, with its special saloon, over the Highland system as desired, and many notable personalities travelled in it at various times, among them King Edward VII and Kaiser Wilhelm of Germany (of course before World War I). It was not used after about 1920, and remained at Dunrobin until 1952 when it came south and was preserved on the premises of the Romney, Hythe & Dymchurch Railway at New Romney. In 1965 it was sold to a Canadian businessman in Victoria, Canada. Now preserved at the Fort Steele Museum, Cranbrooke, British Columbia.

GNR(I) 2–4–2T No 93

1895

Driving wheels: 5ft 7in
Weight: 46 tons 2 cwt
Cylinders: 16in × 22in
Pressure: 175lb
Tractive effort: 12,504lb
Gauge: 5ft 3in

Built at Dundalk works in 1895, (works No 16), GNR No 93 *Sutton,* lost its name during World War I. Withdrawn from service in 1955, it now rests in Belfast Museum, but in the later black livery of the GNR, neither the old green livery or the name having been restored. The illustration shows the engine in its original condition.

Metropolitan Railway Class E 0–4–4T No L44   1896

Driving wheels: 5ft 6in
Weight: 54½ tons
Cylinders: 17¼in×26in
Pressure: 160lb
Tractive effort: 15,000lb

Metropolitan Railway No 1 (replacing the original Beyer Peacock 4–4–0T of 1864 bearing the same number), built at Neasden in 1896. Became London Transport No L44 in 1938, it was one of the small stud of steam engines retained for departmental duties after the LNER took over the passenger workings between Rickmansworth, Aylesbury and Verney Junction. It was used on several occasions in the 1950s on rail-tour specials, and on withdrawal was acquired by the London Railway Preservation Society, now the Quainton Railway Society Ltd. In its LT livery as No L44 it is being restored to working order at the time of writing. It may revert to its former style as Metropolitan No 1.

SER Stirling Class 01 0–6–0 No 65   1896

Driving wheels: 5ft 1in
Weight: 41 tons 1 cwt
Cylinders: 18in × 26in
Pressure: 150lb
Tractive effort: 17,610lb

The only surviving engine built by James Stirling for the South Eastern Railway, and the only one from that company before the 1899 amalgamation into the SE&CR. Built in 1896 with typical Stirling domeless boiler and rebuilt by Wainwright in 1908. SER and SE&CR No 65, it became SR No A65, later No 1065 at the Grouping; and finally BR No 31065. Withdrawn in 1961, then the last of its class, and since acquired privately for preservation. It has been restored to SE&CR livery but is not at present on public display.

LSWR Drummond 0–4–4T 1897

Driving wheels: 5ft 7in
Weight: 60 tons
Cylinders: 18½in × 26in
Pressure: 175lb
Tractive effort: 19,755lb

Dugald Drummond's suburban passenger tank design resulted in 105 engines being built between 1897 and 1911. They remained practically unaltered throughout their existence. No 245 was the fourth engine of this class, turned out from Nine Elms in 1897. It became SR No 245 and BR No 30245, withdrawn from service in 1962 and now awaiting restoration at the National Railway Museum, York. Another engine of the class, No 53, has gone to the Steamtown Museum, USA.

CR 0–4–4T No 419 1897

Driving wheels: 5ft 9in
Weight: 54 tons
Cylinders: 18in × 26in
Pressure: 180lb
Tractive effort: 18,680lb

One of McIntosh's enlarged 0–4–4Ts design of 1897. No 419 was built in 1907, and became LMS No 15189 in 1923, and BR No 55189 in 1948. It was withdrawn from service in 1962. It was acquired by the Scottish Railway Preservation Society and restored to CR livery, and is now housed in their museum at Falkirk. It took part in the 150th Anniversary procession at Shildon in August 1975.

GNR 0–6–0ST No 1247

Driving wheels: 4ft 8in
Weight: 51 tons 14 cwt
Cylinders: 18in×26in
Pressure: 170lb
Tractive effort: 21,735lb

Ivatt's standard shunting tank of 1897, a development of Stirling's original design of 1874. No 1247 was built by Sharp Stewart & Co in 1899 (works No 4492). It became LNER No 4247, and was renumbered 8846 in 1946; finally becoming BR No 68846. It was withdrawn from BR service in 1959, when it was purchased by Capt W. G. Smith. After several moves it has found a home with the national collection.

Taff Vale Railway 0–6–2T

Driving wheels: 4ft 6½in
Weight: 56 tons 8 cwt
Cylinders: 17½in×26in
Pressure: 150lb
Tractive effort: 18,620lb

Taff Vale No 28, built in 1897 at the company's own works in Cardiff, became GWR No 450 at the Grouping, was sold in 1927 for use on the Longmoor Military Railway. Numbered 205 (later 70205) and named *Gordon*. Sold again in 1947 to the Hetton Colliery, becoming No 67. Withdrawn in 1960, presented to British Railways for preservation and now in the former Rhymney Railway works at Caerphilly. A very similar engine, TVR No 85, GWR No 426, was withdrawn in 1927 and sold in 1929 to the Lambton Hetton & Joicey Colliery, where it ran until 1967. It is now on the K&WVR awaiting restoration.

Alexandra Docks Railway 0–4–0ST No 1340

Driving wheels: 3ft 0in
Weight: 22 tons 17 cwt
Cylinders: 12½in×19¾in
Pressure: 120lb
Tractive effort: 8,740lb

Trojan, built for the Alexandra (Newport & South Wales) Docks and Railway by the Avonside Engine Co in 1897 (works No 1386), became GWR No 1340 and was withdrawn from service in 1932. In 1934 it was sold to the Victoria Colliery, Wellington; it later worked at the Netherseal Colliery, Leicestershire. In 1947 it was bought by Alders Paper Mills, Tamworth, where it worked until 1967. Ac-quired for private preservation by Mr J. True, and now to be found at Didcot Railway Centre.

GNR 4–4–2 No 990 'Henry Oakley' 1898

Driving wheels: 6ft 8in
Weight: 60 tons
Cylinders: 19in × 24in
Pressure: 170lb
Tractive effort: 15,649lb

The first Atlantic, or 4–4–2 tender engine in the country. Designed by H. A. Ivatt and built at Doncaster in 1898. It was later rebuilt with a superheater and an extended smokebox, and became LNER No 3990. It was distinguished for many years as the only Great Northern engine to bear a name, having been christened *Henry Oakley*. (It was not until the very end of that company's existence that No 1470 *Great Northern* appeared in 1922). Withdrawn in 1937, it was repainted in GNR colours, and placed in the original York Museum. It was on loan between 1977 and June 1978 to the K&WVR after which it returned to the National Railway Museum, York.

Cardiff Railway 0–4–0ST No 1338 1898

Driving wheels: 3ft 2½in
Weight: 25½ tons
Cylinders: 14in × 21in
Pressure: 160lb
Tractive effort: 14,540lb

Built by Kitson & Son, Leeds in 1898 (works No 3799), this engine, Cardiff Railway No 5, became GWR No 1338 at the Grouping.
    It was one of a pair, the other being No 6, GWR No 1339, scrapped as long ago as 1934, which made the continued survival of No 1338, as an 'odd' engine, somewhat strange.

As BR No 1338 it did in fact remain in service until 1963, and on withdrawal it was preserved privately by the Yieldingtree Museum Trust, now the Somerset Railway Museum. It is now owned by B. K. Kinsey and J. True. The illustration shows the engine shunting at Swansea in 1963. It may be transferred to the Didcot Railway Centre.

LSWR electric shunter   1898

Siemens four-wheel electric locomotive built in 1898 for shunting stock on the Waterloo & City underground line. No DS75, in the Southern Railway's departmental list, was withdrawn in May 1968 and placed in store at Preston Park. Moved to the National Railway Museum at York in November 1977. The current pick-up shoe for third-rail 750V was altered from centre live rail to outside third-rail when the line was re-equipped. The illustration shows the locomotive at an open day at Brighton station.

LBSCR 0–6–2T No 473 'Birch Grove'   1898

had received the name *Princess*, but this was of course removed when the engine was restored as North Stafford No 2. It was one of the last four engines built for the railway, and which actually did not appear until after the Grouping, in the early months of 1923. They did however, carry NSR livery for a time before being repainted LMS black. The L class, as these engines were known, was originally introduced by J. H. Adams in 1903, and 34 of them were eventually constructed. After being repainted, No 2 resumed work at the colliery for a few years, but has now been retired and has gone to Staffordshire County Museum at Shugborough.

GWR Class 5101/6100 2–6–2T   1903

Driving wheels: 5ft 8in
Weight: 78 tons 9 cwt
Cylinders: 18in×30in
Pressure: 200lb
Tractive effort: 24,300lb
The 6100 class had 225lb pressure and TE 27,340lb

Standard GWR express passenger tank class introduced by Churchward in 1903 and perpetuated, with some increase in dimensions, up to 1949. One of the later developments was the 5101 class, the first of which appeared in 1929, eventually comprising Nos 5101-5199 and 4100-4179. The rather larger 6100 class No 6100-6169, came out between 1931 and 1935. Of the latter, No 6106, built at Swindon in 1932, is preserved by the Great Western Society at Didcot together with No 4144. Nos 4141, 4150 and 5164 are all on the Severn Valley Railway at varying stages of restoration. The Great Western Preservation Group owns No 4110 which is being restored in the home counties for eventual use on the Dart Valley Railway, and No 4160 is with the Standard Gauge Steam Trust at Tyseley. No 5193 is at the Steamport Museum, Southport.

GWR Churchward Class 28xx 2–8–0 1903

Driving wheels: 4ft 7½in
Weight: 75½ tons
Cylinders: (2) 18in×30in
Pressure: 225lb
Tractive effort: 35,380lb

This design, introduced in 1903, was the first of the 2–8–0 wheel arrangements in this country. In many ways it could be said to be somewhat ahead of its time, remaining the standard GWR heavy freight engine to the end of that company's existence. By 1919 84 had been built, and after a lapse of nearly 20 years construction was again resumed, another 83 being produced between 1938 and 1942. No 2818, was one of the original batch, having been built in 1905 at Swindon. It is now in the National Railway Museum, York. Another of the class, No 2857, is on the Severn Valley Railway and the Great Western Society at Didcot Railway Centre has preserved No 3822. No 2885 may be preserved by the GWR Preservation Group.

NSR 0–6–2T No 2 1903

Driving wheels: 5ft 0in
Weight: 59½ tons
Cylinders: 18½in×26in
Pressure: 175lb

Excluding minor lines which only had a handful of engines, of all the more important railways which were merged into the 'Big Four' at the 1923 Grouping, the North Stafford had the unfortunate distinction of being the first to have its locomotive stock completely liquidated by its new owners. The last of its 196 engines acquired by the LMS was withdrawn as long ago as 1939. Fortunately a few had been sold out of service, chief among them being five of the L class 0–6–2Ts which went to the Lancashire Associated Collieries, Walkden. One of these was repainted a few years ago in full NSR livery for exhibition at Stoke. This was LMS No 2271. At Walkden Colliery it

GNR 4–4–2 No 251

Driving wheels: 6ft 8in
Weight: 69 tons 12 cwt
Cylinders: 20in × 24in
Pressure: 170lb
Tractive effort: 17,340lb

The first engine of Ivatt's enlarged Atlantic design, built at Doncaster in 1902, it was subsequently rebuilt with superheater but otherwise unchanged. It became LNER No 3251 (for a short time No 251N) at the Grouping, and renumbered 2800 in 1946. Withdrawn in 1947, restored to GNR livery and placed in York Museum. It was temporarily brought out of retirement in 1953 and worked a few special trains in company with its predecessor No 990 (see page 55).

W&LLR 0–6–0T

1902

Driving wheels: 2ft 9in
Weight: 19 tons
Cylinders: 11½in × 16in
Pressure: 150lb
Gauge: 2ft 6in

Two engines were built for the Welshpool & Llanfair Light Railway by Beyer Peacock & Co in 1903 (works Nos 4396 and 4397): No 1 *The Earl* and No 2 *Countess* (originally *The Countess*). After being taken over by the Cambrian Railways they became GWR Nos 822 and 823 at the Grouping, and passed as such into the hands of BR. Passenger services were discontinued in 1931, but freight trains continued until 1956, when the line was closed entirely. It has subsequently been largely reopened by the WLLR PS, and the two engines, which had been laid aside in Oswestry Works, again brought into use. The illustration shows *The Countess*. It ran as just *Countess* from 1923 until recently restored in Cambrian Railway livery. No 1 is currently on long term loan to the National Railway Museum.

NER electric Bo-Bo No 26500

1902

Weight: 46 tons
Tractive effort: 25,000lb

The two original electric locomotives introduced by the NER, built by Brush in 1902, and were both in service until 1965. They were equipped for both overhead and third-rail traction 630V. As NER No 1 and 2, they became Nos 6480 and 6481 in 1946, and eventually BR Nos 26500 and 26501, latterly having been repainted in old NER livery. No 26500 was at first preserved in Leicester Stoneygate Museum. It is now displayed at the National Railway Museum, York in NER livery as No 1.

MR 4—4—0 compound No 1000

1902

Driving wheels: 7ft 0in
Weight: (engine) 61 tons 14 cwt
Cylinders: (1) 19in×26in; (2) 21in×26in
Pressure: 200lb
Tractive effort of low pressure cylinder at 80% boiler pressure: 21,840lb

The first of S. W. Johnson's three-cylinder compounds, built in 1902 as No 2631, and rebuilt by Fowler in 1914 to its present form. It became MR No 1000 in 1907, LMS No 1000 in 1923, and BR No M1000 in 1948; finally becoming No 41000 in 1949. It ran in ordinary service until 1951, then was laid aside at Crewe. It was restored to MR livery in 1959, and put in working order to run enthusiasts' specials until 1962, when it was placed on exhibition in Clapham Museum. Since the closure of Clapham it has been moved to the National Railway Museum, York. It took part in the 150th Centenary procession at Shildon in August, 1975, and has since also been used for enthusiasts' specials.

GWR 'Star' Class 4–6–0 No 4003 'Lode Star'

1906

Driving wheels: 6ft 8½in
Weight: 75 tons 12 cwt
Cylinders: (4) 15in × 26in
Pressure: 225lb
Tractive effort: 27,800lb

Churchward's original four-cylinder design of 1906 (the first engine No 4000 was first built as an Atlantic, but later converted to 4–6–0). No 4003 *Lode Star* was one of the earliest of the class, built in 1907, and one of the last in service. Withdrawn in 1951, it has been preserved in the Great Western Railway Museum at Swindon.

GWR Class 45xx 2–6–2T

1906

Driving wheels: 4ft 7½in
Weight: 57 tons
Cylinders: 17in × 24in
Pressure: 200lb
Tractive effort: 21,250lb

Standard Great Western Railway passenger tank for cross-country work and branch lines, 175 of them having been built between 1906 and 1929. No 4555 was built at Swindon in 1924, and on withdrawal in 1963 was purchased privately. It has been joined on the Dart Valley Railway by No 4588 of the slightly enlarged class, with sloping side tanks. A similar engine, No 5572, has been acquired by the Great Western Society at Taunton and the Norchard Steam Centre has No 5541. Of the original series, No 4566, is on the Severn Valley Railway and Nos 4561, 5521 and 5542

have been acquired by the West Somerset Railway, and await restoration.

SE&CR Wainwright 0–4–4T No 263

1904

Driving wheels: 5ft 6in
Weight: 54 tons 8 cwt
Cylinders: 18in × 26in
Pressure: 160lb
Tractive effort: 17,360lb

Wainwright's standard design of suburban tank engine for the SE&CR. No 263 was built at Ashford in 1904. It became SR No A263 at the Grouping, No 1263 in 1932, and finally BR No 31263. Withdrawn from service in 1964 and acquired by the H Class Trust. It has been restored to SE&CR livery. It is now on the Bluebell Railway.

Metropolitan Railway electric No 5 'John Hampden'

1905

Driving wheels: 3ft 7½in
Weight (as rebuilt): 61½ tons
Maximum tractive effort: 22,600lb

One of the first of 10 locomotives built by the British Westinghouse Electrical & Manufacturing Co Ltd in 1905. They originally had control cabs with sloping equipment compartments at either end. Ten further locomotives were built by British Thomson-Houston in 1906, this time with separate end driving compartments. All 20 were completely reconstructed by Metropolitan Vickers in the early 1920s with more powerful motors, and bow-ended twin driving cabs. Most of them worked until September 1961, when the operation of locomotive-hauled trains was discontinued, although four of them were retained for departmental shunting duties. No 5, *John Hampden* is preserved in the London Transport Museum at Covent Garden. The illustration shows it in ordinary service at Neasden in 1951. No 12 *Sarah Siddons* is still in LT departmental service.

repainted in the old GWR colours with brown underframes, and its original number 3440, and put into ordinary service, usually between Didcot and Southampton. When not so engaged it was used on various special railtours, visiting many parts of the country, including Scotland, during the ensuing few years. These pleasant excursions came to an end in 1963, when the engine was once again retired, this time presumably permanently, and now rests in Swindon Museum. It now again has its 3717 number. The illustration shows the locomotive at Cardiff's Canton shed in 1957.

BCDR Beyer Peacock 4–4–2T No 30   1901

Driving wheels: 5ft 7in
Weight: 56¾ tons
Cylinders: 17in×24in
Pressure: 160lb
Tractive effort: 14,292lb
Gauge: 5ft 3in

Built by Beyer Peacock & Co in 1901 (works No 4231) one of 12 engines, the only really standard class among the BCDR miscellaneous assortment of 30 locomotives, which embraced no less than 11 different types. It became Ulster Transport Authority No 230, but when the remnants of the line became fully dieselised in 1956 it was laid aside for preservation, and now rests, fully restored to BCDR livery in Belfast Museum.

Port Talbot Railway Hudswell Clarke 0–6–0ST No 813   1901

Driving wheels: 4ft 0in
Weight: 44 tons
Cylinders: 16in×24in
Pressure: 160lb
Tractive effort: 17,410lb

Port Talbot Railway No 26, built by Hudswell Clarke & Co in 1901 (works No 555), later becoming GWR No 813. She was sold to the Backworth Colliery in 1901 as its No 12, and renumbered 11 by the National Coal Board. She was withdrawn from service in 1967 and purchased privately for preservation by the 813 Preservation Fund and is now on the Severn Valley Railway.

SE&CR Wainwright Class D 4–4–0 No 737   1901

Driving wheels: 6ft 8in
Weight: 50 tons
Cylinders: 19in × 26in
Pressure: 175lb
Tractive effort: 17,450lb

Wainwright's handsome 4–4–0 design of 1901. Many were later completely rebuilt by Maunsell with superheaters, but a number remained virtually unaltered to the end. No

737 was built at Ashford in 1901, became SR No A737, later No 1737, and finally BR No 31737. Withdrawn in 1956 and laid aside for preservation, at first in Ashford works yard and later sent to Tweedmouth, Northumberland. Finally restored in 1960 to its original condition. After several years in Clapham Museum, it has been transferred to the National Railway Museum, York.

GWR 4–4–0 No 3717 'City of Truro'   1901

Driving wheels: 6ft 8½in
Weight: 55 tons 6 cwt
Cylinders: 18in × 26in
Pressure: 200lb
Tractive effort: 17,790lb

One of Dean's 4–4–0 express design of 1901, *City of Truro* achieved world-wide fame as being the first engine to attain 100mph. Sub-

sequent analysis has thrown some doubt on this figure, but nevertheless there can be no doubt that a hitherto unattained speed of something in the region of 100mph was achieved. Originally built as No 3440, in 1903, numbered 3717 in 1911, and superheated in the same year. It was placed in York Museum on withdrawal, where it remained until early 1957, when it was brought out of retirement,

GER Holden 0–6–0 No 1217E   1901

Driving wheels: 4ft 11in
Weight: 45 tons 8 cwt
Cylinders: 19in×26in
Pressure: 180lb
Tractive effort: 24,340lb

James Holden's freight design of 1901 resulted in 90 engines of this class being built. No 1217 was turned out from Stratford in 1905, and became LNER No 8217 (at first 1217E) at the Grouping. She was renumbered 5567 in 1946 and finally BR No 65567. Withdrawn from ser-

vice in 1962, being the last of the class to remain. Her final duty was in connection with a rail-tour special in the Norwich area in 1962, organised by the Railway Correspondence & Travel Society. Now located at Bressingham Hall, Diss. Originally built with a round topped boiler (LNER Class J16) she had by 1923 acquired a Belpaire firebox (LNER Class J17), which is the reason she cannot be restored with accuracy to GER colours and has therefore been repainted in her first LNER guise.

SE&CR Wainwright 0–6–0 No 592   1900

Driving wheels: 5ft 2in
Weight: 43 tons 16 cwt
Cylinders: 18½in×26in
Pressure: 160lb
Tractive effort: 19,520lb

H. Wainwright's general purpose engine for the SE&CR, of which 106 were built between 1900 and 1908. Practically unaltered throughout their existence, with one exception which was converted to a saddle tank, apart from the provision of shorter chimneys and other details. The last two survivors of the class, of which this was one, were transferred to the Service Department in 1963 and shunted at Ashford until 1967. No 592, built at Longhedge in 1901, became SR No A592, BR No 31592 and finally DS No 239. It has been acquired by Wainwright 'C' Preservation Society

and has been restored to its original condition and can be seen on the Bluebell Railway.

GNR(I) 4–4–0 No 131

1899

Driving wheels: 6ft 7in
Weight: 49 tons
Cylinders: 18½in × 26in
Pressure: 175lb
Tractive effort: 16,755lb
Gauge: 5ft 3in

Built by Neilson & Co in 1900 (works No 5757), this engine was one of a class of 13 engines turned out in 1899 and 1904 as Nos 120-125 and 130-136 of Class Q. No 131, which formerly bore the name *Uranus*, was rebuilt with a higher pitched boiler and superheater in 1920, as Class QS having lost its name about 1914. Transferred to the Coras Iompair Eireann in 1958, when the entire locomotive stock was divided between the CIE and Ulster Transport Authority. It ran until the end of steam on the CIE in the early 1960s since when it has been retained for preservaton. It is seen as preserved on Dundalk station.

BP&GVR 0–6–0ST No 2

1900

Driving wheels: 3ft 6in
Weight: 29 tons
Cylinders: 14in × 20in

No 2 *Pontyberem* of the small BP&GVR in South Wales was a 0–6–0ST built by the Avonside Engine Co in 1900, works No 1421. It was sold in 1914 to Messrs Llewellyn (Nixon) Ltd, later the Mountain Ash Colliery, where it

worked for many years, at least as late as 1949, but later transferred by the National Coal Board to Penrikyber Colliery, where it was in service until 1969. It has now been acquired by the Great Western Society and is at Didcot Railway Centre. As it was disposed of by the BP&GVR as early as 1914 it never became a GWR engine, as did those existing at the 1923 Grouping.

Driving wheels: 3ft 6in
Weight: 26 tons 3 cwt
Cylinders: 14in × 20in
Pressure: 140lb
Tractive effort: 11,105lb

Built in 1906 by the Brush Electrical Engineering Co Ltd of Loughborough (works No 314), this engine became GWR No 921. It was sold to Sugar Beet and Crop Driers Ltd of Eynsham in 1928, and resold to Berry Wiggins & Co Ltd of Kingsnorth, Kent in 1931, where it worked until withdrawal. The photograph was taken in March 1949. It was one of the last engines built by Brush and in view of its special local historic interest has been acquired by the Leicester Museum authorities for exhibition at the Abbey Pumping Station.

NER Class J27 0–6–0 No 2392   1906

Driving wheels: 4ft 7¼in
Weight: 47 tons
Cylinders: 18½in × 26in
Pressure: 180lb
Tractive effort: 24,640lb

The last of a series of large 0–6–0s designed by W. Worsdell, and developed by Raven in 1921 with superheater and piston valves, a total of 115 engines. The last 10 emerged from Darlington after the Grouping in 1923, and No 2392 was the final one of the whole class. Later the superheater was removed. It became No 5894 with the 1946 renumbering scheme, and finally BR No 65894. Withdrawn from service 1967, it has been purchased by the North Eastern Locomotive Preservation Group for use on the North Yorkshire Moors Railway. It has been restored to NER livery as No 2392 and is at present on loan to the National Railway Museum at York.

LT&SR 4–4–2T No 80 'Thundersley'   1909

Driving wheels: 6ft 6in
Weight: 70 tons 15 cwt
Cylinders: 19in × 26in
Pressure: 170lb
Tractive effort: 17,390lb

One of the last four of Whitelegg's final enlarged design of 4–4–2T. Built in 1909 by Stephenson & Co (works No 3367). It became MR No 2177 in 1912, losing its name, and being repainted in MR crimson lake livery. Renumbered 2148 in 1929, it became BR No 41966 in 1948. Withdrawn from service and restored to LT&SR colours in 1956, although not in exact original condition, the chief differences being the extended smokebox. It

Welsh Highland Railway 2–6–2T 'Russell' 1906

Driving wheels: 2ft 4in
Weight: 19 tons 16 cwt
Cylinders: 10¾in × 15in
Pressure: 160lb
Gauge: 1ft 11½in

One of the locomotives owned by the ill-fated Welsh Highland Railway (opened in 1922, and incorporating the much older North Wales Narrow Gauge Railway, and closed in 1937). Built by the Hunslet Engine Co in 1906 (works No 901), it worked until the WHR was closed in 1937, after which it was stored at Dinas until 1941, when it was sold to the Brymbo Steel Co, Wrexham, and in 1943 was at work at Hook Norton, Oxfordshire. In 1948 it came into possession of Messrs Fayles, of Corfe Castle, Wareham, Dorset, and on the closure of that line in 1955 was acquired by the Birmingham Locomotive Club and placed on exhibition at the Talyllyn Railway's museum at Towyn. It has recently undergone some restoration and has gone to the Welsh Highland Preservation Society's new headquarters at Porthmadog.

Powlesland & Mason Ltd 0–4–0ST No 6 1906

GWR Class 1361 0–6–0ST No 1363

Driving wheels: 3ft 8in
Weight: 35 tons 4 cwt
Cylinders: 16in×20in
Pressure: 150lb
Tractive effort: 14,835lb

One of five shunting engines built at Swindon in 1910. Withdrawn from service in 1962, it has been acquired by the Great Western Society Ltd; it is now at the Didcot Railway Centre.

GWR Class 42xx 2–8–0T

Driving wheels: 4ft 7½in
Weight: 81 tons 12 cwt
Cylinders: 18½in×30in
Pressure: 200lb
Tractive effort: 31,450lb

A type of heavy tank engine introduced by Churchward for short-distance mineral traffic, principally in the South Wales coalfields. In all 205 engines were built between 1910 and 1940, Nos 4200-4299, 5200-5294, and a second lot bearing the Nos 5255-5264, to replace the originals of these numbers which, together with Nos 5265-5294, had been rebuilt as 2–8–2Ts. No 5239 has been restored and now works on the Dart Valley Railway's Torbay line and is now named *Goliath*. No 5224 has been moved from Barry to the Main Line Steam Trust for preservation, and No 4270 has been acquired for the Swansea Industrial and Maritime Museum.

GCR Robinson 2–8–0 No 102

worked a special commemorative train from Southend to Liverpool Street on 3 March 1956, and was subsequently put into storage at Derby. The illustration shows the engine at Bressingham.

SE&CR Wainwright Class P 0–6–0T 1910

Driving wheels: 3ft 9in
Weight: 28½ tons
Cylinders: 12in × 18in
Pressure: 160lb
Tractive effort: 7,810lb

Eight engines, of which four have been preserved, were built by H. S. Wainwright in 1909/10 for railmotor work, latterly used on light shunting duties.

SECR Nos	SR Nos	BR Nos	Fate
27*	A27/1027	31027	Sold to Bluebell Railway 1961
178†	A178/1178	178S/31178	Sold to Bowaters, Sittingbourne in 1958. Now on Bluebell Railway, repainted as SR 1178
323‡	A323/1323	31323	Sold to Bluebell Railway 1960
753/556**	A556/1556	31556	Sold to Hodsons Mills, Robertsbridge, 1960. Now K&ESR No 11

*Formerly named *Primrose*, now restored to SE&CR livery.
†Formerly named *Pioneer II*.
‡Now named *Bluebell*.
**Formerly named *Pride of Sussex*.

livery under its BR number 69023, and named *Joem*. After several years in the K&WVR it went to the Yorkshire Dales Railway, but in 1977 it was purchased by the Derwent Valley Light Railway, York, for use on its newly introduced passenger service, which terminated in August 1979, and the locomotive and coaches disposed of. The locomotive is illustrated at Layerthorpe station in June 1978.

CR 0–6–0 No 828

Driving wheels: 5ft 0in
Weight: 45 tons 14 cwt
Cylinders: 18½in×26in
Pressure: 160lb
Tractive effort: 20,169lb

One of McIntosh's 1899 design of 0–6–0 for the Caledonian Railway. No 828 was built in the Company's own workshops at St Rollox in that year. It became LMS No 17566 in 1923, BR No 57566 in 1948. It was withdrawn from service in 1963. Restored to CR livery, it is at present on loan to the Glasgow Transport Museum. It is the property of the Scottish Locomotive Preservation Trust Fund.

LSWR Class T9 4–4–0 No 120

Driving wheels: 6ft 1in
Weight: 51 tons 18 cwt
Cylinders: 19in×26in
Pressure: 175lb
Tractive effort: 17,675lb

Dugald Drummond's most successful express passenger class. Although almost the earliest, they outlasted all their later successors. Between 1899 and 1901 66 engines were built, of which No 120 was one of the first, being turned out from Nine Elms in 1899. All were eventually rebuilt by Urie with extended smokebox and superheaters, No 120 being so treated in 1927. It became SR No 120 at the Grouping, and BR No 30120 at Nationalisation. Withdrawn in 1963, the last to remain in traffic, it was repainted in LSWR 1918 livery and worked for a time on enthusiasts' specials. The illustration shows the engine as restored in LSWR colours, although it never actually ran thus in this particular condition. For a time on loan to the Standard Gauge Steam Trust, Tyseley, it has now joined the National Railway Museum's collection at York.

Driving wheels: 5ft 0in
Weight: 57½ tons
Cylinders: 17½in×26in
Pressure: 170lb
Tractive effort: 19,175lb

Built in 1898, one of R. Billinton's numerous class of E4 0–6–2Ts for suburban passenger work, it was reboilered in 1912, acquiring an extended smokebox and other modifications. Originally LBSCR *Birch Grove* it became SR

No 2473 at the Grouping (having lost its name for many years), then at first BR No 2473S on Nationalisation and finally No 32473. Withdrawn from service in 1962 and acquired by the Bluebell Railway, it was repainted in the chocolate brown livery introduced by Marsh in 1905. It could therefore never have actually run on the LBSCR in this particular condition, as apart from having lost its original yellow livery (and brass number plate) it was not rebuilt with its present boiler until 1912.

Groudle Glen Miniature Railway 2–4–0T 1898

Gauge: 1ft 11½in

One of two small 2–4–0Ts built by Bagnall & Co for the Groudle Glen Miniature Railway on the Isle of Man. *Sea Lion* was built in 1898 (works No 1484) and *Polar Bear* in 1908 (1781). The line became disused during World War II. It was reopened 1950-1958 and 1961/2, but thereafter closed completely. The engines were still in store in 1964. *Polar Bear* is now preserved at Brockham Museum, Surrey, and *Sea Lion* at Kirkmichael Steam Centre, Isle of Man. Another similar engine at Brockham is *Peter* – Bagnall 1917 (works No 2067) from the Cliffe Hill Granite Co, Leicester, property of the Narrow Gauge Railway Society. The illustration shows *Polar Bear* at work in the Isle of Man in 1961.

NER Class J72 0–6–0T No 69023 1898

Driving wheels: 4ft 1¼in
Weight: 38 tons
Cylinders: 17in×24in
Pressure: 140lb
Tractive effort: 16,760lb

Although of North Eastern design, this particular engine was built by BR in 1951. There is no other comparable instance of a design having been built unchanged over a period of 53 years, under three different ownerships and four locomotive superintendencies. The type was originally introduced by Wilson Worsdell in 1898. It is perhaps unfortunate that none of the original NER engines was still in existence for preservation, but one of the last post-Nationalisation engines was acquired by the Keighley & Worth Valley Preservation Society. Built as BR No 69023 in 1951, it was latterly transferred to the departmental list as No 59, being withdrawn in 1966. It has been repainted in North Eastern

with slight modifications. Rebuilt by Gresley with round-topped boiler, LNER Class B12/3, it was renumbered 1572 in 1946 and became BR No 61572. Withdrawn in 1961, the last GER design of 4–6–0 in service, it was acquired by the Midland and Great Northern Joint Preservation Society, now the North Norfolk Railway Society Ltd. The illustration shows the engine in its 1971 condition, prior to the commencement of restoration.

GWR Class 43xx 2–6–0   1911

Driving wheels: 5ft 8in
Weight: 62 tons
Cylinders: 18½in × 30in
Pressure: 200lb
Tractive effort: 25,670lb

Churchward's very successful design of mixed traffic 2–6–0, of which 342 were built between 1911 and 1932, numbered variously in the 4300, 5300, 6300, 7300, 8300 and 9300 series. Two have survived. No 5322, built at Swindon in 1932, has been purchased by the Great Western Society, and is now to be found at their Didcot Railway Centre. Another of the class, No 9303 (later No 7325), has been rescued from Barry scrapyard by the Severn Valley Railway.

CDR 2–6–4T No 2   1912

Driving wheels: 4ft 0in
Weight: 50 tons 8 cwt
Cylinders: 15½in × 21in
Pressure: 160lb
Tractive effort: 14,295lb
Gauge: 3ft 0in

Built by Nasmyth Wilson in 1921 (works No 956) as No 2A *Stranorlar*. Became No 2 *Blanche* in 1928. Withdrawn in 1959 on closure of the line, and is now at rest in Belfast Museum. Another somewhat similar engine No 6 *Columbkille* – Nasmyth Wilson 1907 (works No 830) originally purchased together with two others for transportation to the USA, has now been acquired by the North West of Ireland Society, who hope to operate it on a short length of preserved railway possibly at Shane's Castle, Antrim.

Driving wheels: 4ft 8in
Weight: 73 tons 4 cwt
Cylinders: (2) 21in×26in
Pressure: 180lb
Tractive effort: 31,325lb

J. G. Robinson's very successful design of mineral engine for the GCR, introduced in 1911. It was adopted as a standard type for overseas work by the Railway Operating Division during World War I, and several hundred were built, apart from those actually constructed for the Great Central Railway. Many of these subsequently came into the hands of the LNER, whilst some were sold abroad. One of the originals built at Gorton in 1911, No 102, which became LNER No 5102 at the Grouping, was renumbered 3509 in 1946 and No 3601 in 1947, and finally BR No 63601, remained in its original condition. It was withdrawn from service in 1963, and is now at the Dinting Railway Centre, Glossop.

MR Class 4 Goods No 43924   1911

Driving wheels: 5ft 3in
Weight: 48¾ tons
Cylinders: 20in×26in
Pressure: 175lb
Tractive effort: 24,555lb

Sir Henry Fowler's 1911 design of freight engine for the MR of which 192 were built up to the Grouping in 1923. The design was adopted as standard for new construction by the LMS. No fewer than 575 further engines were built between 1924 and 1941, plus another five for the Somerset & Dorset Joint Railway. No 3924 was built at Derby in 1920 as No 8 of order 5335. Withdrawn in 1965 as BR No 43924, it was sent to a scrapyard in South Wales, but was fortunately still in existence in 1968 when the Midland 4F Preservation Society successfully sought its purchase. It now runs on the

K&WVR in the first British Railway's livery as No 43924.

GER Class B12 4–6–0 No 61572   1911

Driving wheels: 6ft 6in
Weight: 69½ tons
Cylinders: 20in×28in
Pressure: 180lb
Tractive effort: 21,970lb

Not strictly speaking a Great Eastern engine, as it was constructed several years after the Grouping, in 1928, by Beyer Peacock & Co (works No 6488) as LNER No 8572. It was however, of S. D. Holden's design of 1911,

NBR 4–4–0 No 256 'Glen Douglas' 1913

Driving wheels: 6ft 0in
Weight: 57 tons 4 cwt
Cylinders: 20in×26in
Pressure: 165lb
Tractive effort: 20,260lb

W. P. Reid's 'Glen' class, LNER Class D34 introduced in 1913 for more heavily graded routes such as the West Highland Line. No 256 was built at Cowlairs in 1913; it became LNER No 9256 in 1923, renumbered 2469 in 1946 and BR No 62469 at Nationalisation. Withdrawn in 1959 and restored to NBR condition and livery in working order for use on special tours, which it performed for several years. The illustration shows it on one of these occasions at Dawsholm Shed in 1959. Now housed in Glasgow Transport Museum.

S&DJR 2–8–0 1914

Driving wheels: 4ft 8½in
Weight: 64¾ tons
Cylinders: 21in×28in
Pressure: 190lb
Tractive effort: 23,595lb

Eleven engines built to the design of Sir Henry Fowler for use on the Somerset and Dorset Joint Railway, although the parent Midland Railway never had any of its own. The first six, Nos 80-85, came from Derby in 1914, followed

NER Class Q6 0–8–0 No 2238 1913

Driving wheels: 4ft 7½in
Weight: 65 tons 18 cwt
Cylinders: 20in×26in
Pressure: 180lb
Tractive effort: 28,800lb

Raven 0–8–0 mineral engines, developed from Worsdell's 1901 design; 120 engines were built

between 1913 and 1921. No 2238 was built at Darlington in 1918. Renumbered 3395 in 1946, it eventually became BR No 6395. drawal from service in 1967, it was purchased by the North Eastern Locomotive Preservation Group for use on the North Yorkshire Moors Railway. Illustrated as now restored to NER livery as No 2238.

GNR(I) 4–4–0 No 171 'Slieve Gullion' 1913

Driving wheels: 6ft 7in
Weight: 53 tons 6 cwt
Cylinders: 19in×26in
Pressure: 200lb
Tractive effort: 20,198lb
Gauge: 5ft 3in

Originally built by Beyer Peacock & Co in 1913 (works No 5629), and completely renewed at

Dundalk in 1939. As No 171 *Slieve Gullion*, it lost its name in 1925, but this was restored in 1939 when the engine received the new blue livery. On withdrawal in 1965 it was acquired by the Irish Railway Preservation Society, in running order, for use on enthusiasts' specials. It is at present kept at the Society's premises at Whitehead. Here seen heading special out of Antrim on 2 September 1978.

railway, it serves at any rate to perpetuate the memory of a great railway. No 9 was built by the North British Locomotive Co in 1917, renumbered 324 in 1919, and subsequently LMS No 16379. It was sold in 1934 to the Llay Main Collieries, Denbighshire, where it worked until acquired for preservation in 1965. It is now housed in Glasgow Transport Museum, repainted in the old G&SWR livery.

SE&CR Maunsell Class N 2–6–0 No 31874   1917

Driving wheels: 5ft 6in
Weight: 61 tons 4 cwt
Cylinders: 19in × 28in
Pressure: 200lb
Tractive effort: 26,035lb

Maunsell's first design for the SE&CR, after he had come from the GS&WR in Ireland. The outstanding feature of the engine, at that date unappreciated by locomotive engineers in general, with the exception of Churchward on the GWR, was the use of long valve travel. Its significance in improved front end design was henceforth increasingly recognised on other railways.

The initial SE&CR engine, No 810, was followed after extensive trials by further examples, and the design was adopted after the war by the Government for 100 engines to be built at Woolwich Arsenal to relieve unemployment, 50 of which were purchased by the SR. They put in many years of useful service all over the system, but especially in the West of England. The last survivor, No 31874, has been rescued from Barry Scrapyard by the Mid-Hants Railway Preservation Society, which has restored part of the former LSWR line between Alresford and Alton over which the engine now works. It currently carries the name *Brian Fisk*.

NSR 0–4–0 battery locomotive   1917

by Nos 86-90, from R. Stephenson & Co in 1925. These had larger boilers, but they were subsequently rebuilt to conform with the earlier series. This engine was one of the second lot, originally S&DJR No 88. subsequently LMS No 9678 and later No 13808, and finally BR No 53808. Together with its sister engine No 53809, it was withdrawn in 1964 and lay in Barry scrapyard for several years,

to be rescued by the Somerset and Dorset Railway Circle in 1970. At first stored at Radstock, it is now at the premises of the West Somerset Railway at Washford. No 53809 has been purchased by Mr Beaumont and is undergoing restoration at Kirk Smeaton, but will be transferred to the North Yorkshire Moors Railway.

GER Class N7 0–6–2T No 999 — 1914

Driving wheels: 4ft 10in
Weight: 61 tons 16 cwt
Cylinders: 18in×24in
Pressure: 180lb
Tractive effort: 20,515lb

Again not perhaps a true Great Eastern engine (see remarks on page 73 regarding the B12 4–6–0), having been built in 1924 as LNER No 999E, it was nevertheless of Hill's GER design of 1914. It duly became LNER No 7999, renumbered 9621 in 1947, and finally BR No 69621. Withdrawn in 1962 and acquired privately for preservation, it is now at the Chappel Steam Centre at Chappel & Wakes Colne and has been restored as GER No 999. These engines performed many years of

useful work on the busy LNER suburban services out of Liverpool Street.

G&SWR 0–6–0T No 9 — 1917

Driving wheels: 4ft 2in
Weight: 40 tons
Cylinders: 17in×22in
Pressure: 160lb
Tractive effort: 17,293lb

Of all the major companies to be absorbed into the four large Groups in 1923, the G&SWR was the second company whose stock of locomotives became completely liquidated (the North Stafford was the first to obtain this dubious distinction); in fact only one engine remained to be taken over by British Railways in 1948. The conception of preservation on a grand scale was at that time only in its infancy, and when in more recent years the idea became generally accepted the prospect of a representative G&SWR engine, to complete the Scottish picture, had become somewhat remote. Fortunately a few G&SWR engines had been sold out of service to industrial concerns; and had the project been proposed more vigorously, only a year or two earlier, when there were still in existence a Manson 0–6–0 tender engine and at least two White-

legg 0–6–2Ts, both very suitable types for preservation, a more satisfactory outcome might have been achieved. Unfortunately by the time the need for a G&SWR engine came to be finally appreciated, these had gone, and the only remaining examples were a couple of 0–6–0Ts, originally three in number, which had been sold to collieries and were still in existence. One of these was secured, and although hardly representative of general G&SWR practice, or indeed of any main line

L&YR petrol tractor No 1

1919

Engine: 4-cylinder petrol engine 30hp

One of three small petrol shunters supplied in 1920 to the Lancashire & Yorkshire Railway, built by Simplex in 1919 (works No 1947). They were sold out of service in 1930, No 1 going to the British Oil & Cake Mills, Hull, later transferred to Greenock, and subsequently acquired by Rylands Wireworks of Warrington, whence it has now been obtained by the Railway Preservation Society, and can be seen at Chasewater.

GNSR 4–4–0 No 49 'Gordon Highlander'

1920

Driving wheels: 6ft 1in
Weight: 48 tons 13 cwt
Cylinders: 18in × 26in
Pressure: 165lb
Tractive effort: 16,185lb

The final design of express engine for the old GNSR. Built by the North British Locomotive

Co in 1920, it became LNER No 6849 in 1923, renumbered 2277 in 1946, and BR No 62277 in 1948. Withdrawn in 1958 and restored to GNSR livery and put in working order for use on special tours, which it performed for several years. It is now housed in Glasgow Museum.

GNR 0–6–2T No 4744

1920

Driving wheels: 5ft 8in
Weight: 70¼ tons
Cylinders: 19in × 26in
Pressure: 170lb
Tractive effort: 19,945lb

Gresley's enlargement of his first 0–6–2T design of 1907 (LNER Class N1). This bigger version was introduced in 1920 (LNER Class N2), mainly for the London suburban services. No 1744 was built by the North British Locomotive Co in 1921, became LNER No 4744, was renumbered 9523 in 1946 and finally BR

Wheels: 3ft 1in

Two BTH motors giving 4bhp on 250volts dc and 108 21-plate cells.

Built by T. Bolton & Sons for the North Stafford Railway in 1917 for use at Oakmoor near Leek.

Withdrawn from service in 1964 and repainted in NSR colours. It is now at Staffordshire County Council Museum at Shugborough Hall, near Stafford.

Talyllyn Railway 0–4–0T No 6   1918

Driving wheels: 21½in
Cylinders: 6¾in × 10¾in
Pressure: 140lb
Tractive effort: 2,710lb
Gauge: 2ft 3in

Built by Andrew Barclay & Sons in 1918 for the Admiralty. Used first at Marston Aerodrome, Kent, transferred in 1921 to the Calshot RAF railway. It was presented to the Talyllyn Railway in 1953 by Abelson & Co Ltd of Birmingham. Now known as No 6 *Douglas*.

NER Raven 0–8–0 No 63460   1919

Driving wheels: 4ft 7¼in
Weight: 71½ tons
Cylinders: (3) 18½in × 26in
Pressure: 180lb
Tractive effort: 36,965lb

The final design of 0–8–0 mineral engine for the NER, of which a large number was constructed between 1901 and 1924. The last 15, LNER Class Q7, were three-cylinder engines, the original No 901 having been built at Dar-

lington in 1919. It passed into LNER hands as No 901, becoming No 3460 under the 1946 renumbering scheme, and eventually BR No 63460. The whole class was withdrawn in 1962, but the initial engine was laid aside for preservation, and actually steamed again in 1963 for working a society's special train from Tyne Dock to Consett. Part of the National collection it is at present on loan to the North Yorkshire Moors Railway.

No 69523. Withdrawn from service in 1962, and secured for preservation by the Gresley Society, it was for some years on the Keighley & Worth Valley Railway, but is now at work on the GCR Main Line Steam Trust, Loughborough. Restored as LNER No 4744.

GCR 'Director' class 4–4–0 No 506 'Butler Henderson'

1920

Driving wheels: 6ft 9in
Weight: 61 tons 3 cwt
Cylinders: 20in×26in
Pressure: 180lb
Tractive effort: 19,645lb

Robinson's very fine 4–4–0 design for the GCR. The first 10 engines, known as LNER Class D10, were built in 1913, and another 11, Class D11/1, of which No 506 was one, followed in 1920.

   Butler Henderson became LNER No 5506 at the Grouping, renumbered 2660 in October 1946, and BR No 62660 in 1948. In LNER days, the small splashers accommodating the coupling rods had been removed and the frames cut away accordingly, but these have now been replaced and the engine restored to its authentic GCR original condition. After several years in Clapham Museum, it has now been loaned by the National Railway Museum to the Main Line Steam Trust, where it is displayed at their Loughborough premises on the former GCR main line.

LSWR Urie Class S15 4–6–0 No 506   1920

Driving wheels: 5ft 7in
Weight: 79¾ tons
Cylinders: 21in×28in
Pressure: 180lb
Tractive effort: 28,200lb

A class of 20 engines built at Eastleigh by R. W. Urie in 1920/1 for fast fitted freight duties, mainly between London and Southampton. They were modelled largely on his express '736' class of 1918 with 6ft 7in driving wheels for express passenger services and later integrated into Maunsell's 'King Arthur' class. The engine was withdrawn from service in January 1964, together with No 499, the last two to remain in traffic, and both of them lay in Barry scrapyard for several years. The Urie S15 Preservation Group has purchased No 30506 and it is currently undergoing rest-

oration to working order and SR green livery, at Ropley on the Mid-Hants Railway.

LNWR Class G2 0–8–0 No 49395   1921

Driving wheels: 4ft 5½in
Weight: 60¼ tons
Cylinders: 20½in×24in
Pressure: 175lb
Tractive effort: 29,015lb

The first of the final design of 0–8–0, Class G2, introduced by Beames in 1921, and a de-

velopment of previous engines of this wheel arrangement built by Webb, Whale, and Bowen-Cooke. It was turned out from Crewe in 1921 as LNWR No 485, became LMS No 9395 and finally No BR 49395. Withdrawn from service in 1959 it is now being restored by the Telford (Horsehay) Steam Trust.

Corris Railway 0–4–2ST No 4 'Edward Thomas'   1921

Driving wheels: 2ft 0in
Cylinders: 7in×12in
Tractive effort: 3,450lb
Gauge: 2ft 3in

Built by Kerr Stuart in 1921 (works No 4047) for the Corris Railway, which was taken over by the GWR in 1930 and in turn by BR in 1948. In that year the line was closed, but in 1951 this engine together with No 3 (see page 31) was acquired by the Talyllyn Railway, on which line it now runs as No 4 *Edward Thomas*. It ran for a time with a Giesl ejector. It is interesting to note that it has carried the same number under its four different ownerships.

LNER Class A3 4–6–2 No 4472 'Flying Scotsman' 1922

Driving wheels: 6ft 8in
Weight: (engine only) 96¼ tons
Cylinders: (3) 19in×26in
Pressure: 220lb
Tractive effort: 32,910lb

Sir Nigel Gresley's first Pacific design of 1922, originally LNER Class A1 subsequently redesignated A10. Later modified with higher pressure boiler as class A3. No 1472N as it was originally, was built at Doncaster in 1923 (works No 1564), and later renumbered 4472

and given the name *Flying Scotsman*. Withdrawn in 1963 as BR No 60103, and acquired privately by Mr Alan Pegler for preservation in running order, it was restored as LNER No 4472. In 1969 it went to the United States, and has made extensive tours in that country and Canada. It returned to the UK in February 1973 and is frequently to be seen on enthusiasts' steam specials over routes approved by BR. It is now owned by Mr William McAlpine and Flying Scotsman Enterprises, and at the time of writing, is housed at Steamtown, Carnforth.

D&SER 2–6–0 No 15 1922

Driving wheels: 5ft 1in
Weight: 50 tons
Cylinders: 19in×26in
Pressure: 175lb
Tractive effort: 22,800lb
Gauge: 5ft 3in

One of two 2–6–0s built for the D&SER as Nos 15 and 16 by Beyer Peacock in 1922, (6112, 6113), they became Great Southern Nos 461

and 462. No 461 ran until the end of steam on CIE in the early 1960s, since when it has been retained for preservation, being restored to D&SER livery, of black, lined out in red and orange, with its old No 15. The illustration shows it as restored. It is hoped that it may be possible for it to be restored to working order for use on steam specials by the Railway Preservation Society of Ireland.

Ravenglass & Eskdale Railway 2–8–2   1923

Driving wheels: 1ft 5½in
Cylinders: 5⅞in×8½in
Gauge: 1ft 3in

Built by Davey Paxman Ltd, Colchester in 1923. Between 1927 and 1935 it ran as an articulated 2–8–2+0–8–0 engine, the second power unit being situated under the tender, but it reverted to its original state in the form in which it now runs, as No 8 *River Esk*. It

should be mentioned that a very similar engine with certain modifications, No 9 *River Mite*, was built in 1966 by Mr H. Clarkson, of York, to the order of the Preservation Society. As this is one of the last new steam locomotives to have been built in this country, it seems that it would be inappropriate, so far as the object of this book is concerned, to describe this as a 'preserved locomotive'.

GWR 'Castle' Class 4–6–0   1923

Driving wheels: 6ft 8½in
Weight: 79 tons 17 cwt
Cylinders: (4) 16in×26in
Pressure: 225lb
Tractive effort: 31,625lb

Collett's famous 'Castle' design of 1923, developed from Churchward's 'Star' class of 1906. The original engine, No 4073 *Caerphilly Castle*, has found an honourable resting place in the Science Museum, Kensington. Others have been preserved, including No 4079 *Pen-*

dennis Castle (which took part in the locomotive exchanges between the GWR and LNER in 1925). In 1976 it was sold to Hammersley Iron and exported to Dampier, Australia for use on their main line on special excursions. No 5051 *Earl Bathurst* is to be found at the Great Western Society's Didcot Railway Centre. It has since been joined by No 5029 *Nunney Castle*. Some of the 'Castles' were fitted with double blast pipes and double chimneys, of which No 7029 *Clun Castle* was

one. This was one of the first engines to be preserved in working order, by the Standard Gauge Steam Trust, with its well-equipped premises at Tyseley, Birmingham. It also has No 7027 *Thornbury Castle*, and with commendable foresight for the future, purchased two other 'Castles' from Barry scrapyard, whilst they were still available, more as a source of spare parts than with a view to restoration; these are Nos 5043 *Earl of Mount Edgecumbe*, and 5080 *Defiant*.

LMS Class 4 0–6–0

1924

Driving wheels: 5ft 3in
Weight: 48¾ tons
Cylinders: 20in×26in
Pressure: 175lb
Tractive effort: 24,555lb

This class, which eventually totalled 580 engines (including five built for the S&DJR), was a direct follow-on of Fowler MR design of 1911 for the Midland Railway, consisting of another 192 engines, (see page 73). No 4027

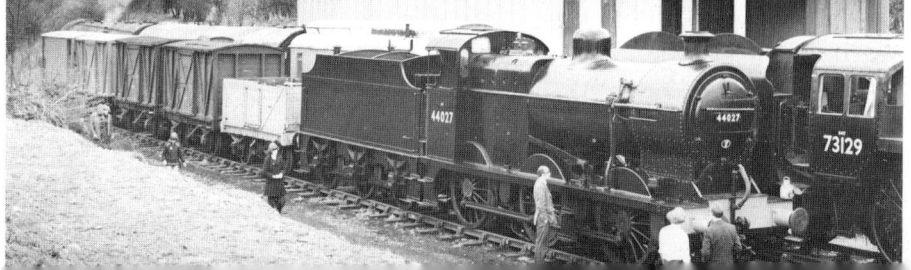

was the first post Grouping engine, being built at Derby in 1924, the first of an order for 30 engines under lot No 6213. As BR No 44027, it was withdrawn from service in 1964 and is now at Butterley headquarters of the Midland Railway Trust, repainted as BR No 44027. No 44422, from Barry scrapyard, acquired by the North Staffordshire Railway Society for use at its headquarters at Cheddleton, on the Churnet Valley line. No 44123, (still at Barry at the time of writing) is a further candidate for preservation.

LMS(NCC) 4–4–0 No 74   1924

Driving wheels: 6ft 0in
Weight: 51½ tons
Cylinders: 19in × 24in
Pressure: 170lb
Tractive effort: 17,388lb
Gauge: 5ft 3in

Built by the North British Locomotive Co in 1924 (works No 23096) to Derby design, for the Irish part of the LMS system, inherited from the Midland Railway. Named *Dunluce Castle* in 1931, withdrawn from service in 1962, and repainted in full MR crimson lake livery, and now in Belfast Museum. The illustration shows it at York Road in 1963.

LMS Class 3F 0–6–0T   1924

Driving wheels: 4ft 7in
Weight: 49½ tons
Cylinders: 18in×26in
Pressure: 160lb
Tractive effort: 20,835lb

This LMS standard design of shunting tank, of which 422 were turned out between 1924 and 1931 (including seven originally built for the Somerset & Dorset), was a direct development of Johnson's 1899 design for the Midland Railway. Four engines have been obtained by the Midland Railway Trust, Butterley, Derby-

shire. These are Nos 47327, 47357, 47445 and 47564 originally LMS Nos 16410, 16440, 16528 and 16647. No 47357 has already been restored as LMS No 16440, in pre-1928 style with large number on the side tanks and in LMS maroon, although these engines never actually carried this livery. Others of the type preserved include No 47279 on the Keighley & Worth Valley Railway; No 47298 at Steamport, Southport; No 47324 on the Mid-Hants Railway; No 47383 on the Severn Valley Railway and No 47493 at Cranmore, on the East Somerset Railway.

GWR Collett Class 56xx 0–6–2T 1924

Driving wheels: 4ft 7½in
Weight: 69 tons 7 cwt
Cylinders: 18in×26in
Pressure: 200lb
Tractive effort: 25,800lb

One of a class of 200 engines built between 1924 and 1928, mainly for service in South Wales to replace the non-standard engines of the former independent railways absorbed into the Great Western. No 6697 was one of the last survivors, being withdrawn in 1966. It is now at Didcot Railway Centre. Others of the class since acquired from Barry include No 5619 by the Telford (Horsehay) Steam Trust, No 5643 at Steamtown, Carnforth, No 5637 at Tyseley, No 6619 on the North Yorkshire Moors Railway and late in 1978 No 6695 was

moved from Barry to Swanage for preservation.

SR 'Lord Nelson' Class 4–6–0 No 30850 1926

Driving wheels: 6ft 7in
Weight: 83½ tons
Cylinders: (4) 18½in×26in
Pressure: 220lb
Tractive effort: 33,510lb

Maunsell's largest express passenger class, built mainly for working the Continental boat trains between Victoria and Dover. The initial engine, No E850 *Lord Nelson*, was built at Eastleigh in 1926, followed by another 15 engines in 1928/9. Except for the last member of the class, these engines were unusual for a four-cylinder type in having the cranks on the driving axle set at 135°, giving eight exhaust beats for each wheel's revolution instead of four beats with the cranks at the customary 90°. Later modifications included the provision of smoke deflectors at the sides of the smoke-box, and a double blast pipe, involving a very ugly wide chimney. The illustration shows

the engine at Eastleigh in 1961. Withdrawn from service in 1962, No 850, part of the national collection, is at Steamtown, Carnforth.

SR 'King Arthur' Class 4–6–0 No 777 'Sir Lamiel'

1925

Driving wheels: 6ft 7in
Weight: 80 tons 19 cwt
Cylinders: 20½in × 28in
Pressure: 200lb
Tractive effort: 25,320lb

Maunsell's very successful express passenger engines, developed from Urie's LSWR design of 1918. Southern Railway No E777 *Sir Lamiel* was built by the North British Locomotive Co in 1925 (works No 23223), later No 777 (without the E prefix) and finally BR No 30777. Withdrawn in 1961, it has been retained for official preservation, and is now to be restored at Hull by the Humberside Locomotive Preservation Group.

LMS Hughes Class 5MT 2–6–0

1926

Driving wheels: 5ft 6in
Weight: 66 tons
Cylinders: 21in × 26in
Pressure: 160lb
Tractive effort: 26,580lb

The first of Hughes' design of mixed traffic 2–6–0 for the LMS, built at Horwich in 1926. The very high running plate was somewhat unusual at the time, but was destined to be a portent of the future trend in locomotive design. Originally No 13000 it was renumbered 2700 in 1934, and then became British Railways No 42700. Withdrawn from service in 1966, it is now at the National Railway Museum, York, after restoration to LMS livery. No 42765, from Barry, is now on the Keighley and Worth Valley Railway.

GWR 'King' Class 4—6—0 1927

Driving wheels: 6ft 6in
Weight: 89 tons
Cylinders: (4) 16¼in×28in
Pressure: 250lb
Tractive effort: 40,300lb

The first of Great Western's largest express passenger engines (except for the solitary and ill-fated Pacific *The Great Bear*) introduced by Collett in 1927, of which 30 examples were built. The original engine made history by visiting the United States of America, and on its return continued to carry the bell with which

it was fitted during its visit. It was withdrawn in 1962 for preservation and placed in store at Swindon. Subsequently, it was returned to working order and placed on loan to Bulmers, the Hereford cider makers, where it formed the nucleus of their railway centre. No 6000 headed an experimental 'return of steam' railtour over BR routes in 1972. It is periodically to be seen working steam excursions over approved routes on the BR system. A second engine of the class No 6024 *King Edward I*, is at Quainton Road undergoing restoration.

LMS Rebuilt 'Royal Scot' Class 4—6—0 1927

Driving wheels: 6ft 9in
Weight: 83 tons
Cylinders: (3) 18in×26in
Pressure: 250lb
Tractive effort: 33,150lb

No 6100 was the first of the well known 'Royal Scot' class, introduced in 1927. It visited the United States of America and Canada in 1933 and covered 11,194 miles over their railroads.

Reconstructed in 1950 with a taper boiler; withdrawn from service in 1962 and restored to LMS livery, although it never actually ran in this particular style, having become BR No 46100 before rebuilding. Now at Bressingham Hall, Diss. Another of the class, No 46115 *Scots Guardsman* (the last to remain in traffic, and withdrawn in 1965) has been privately preserved, and is at the Dinting Railway Centre.

SR Maunsell Class S15 4–6–0 1927

Driving wheels: 5ft 7in
Weight with tender: 79¼ tons
Cylinders: 20½in×28in
Pressure: 200lb
Tractive effort: 29,855lb

Maunsell's development of Urie's 1920 design (see page 82) for express freight work and occasional passenger use, of which 25 engines were built between 1927 and 1936, Nos 823 to 847, later BR Nos 30823 to 30847. No 30841 was saved from Barry scrapyard in 1973 by the Essex Locomotive Society and restored at Chappel & Wakes Colne. It has been restored as SR No 841 in green livery and has been named *Greene King*. It took part in the 150th Anniversary procession at Shildon in August 1975. No 841 worked trains on the Nene Valley Railway during the 1978 season, at the end of which it was transferred to the North York Moors Railway. Another member of the class, No 30847, has been moved from Barry to the Bluebell Railway for preservation.

LNER 0–4–0 Sentinel shunter 1927

Driving wheels: 2ft 6in
Weight: 19 tons 6 cwt
Cylinders: (2 vertical) 6¾in×9in
Pressure: 275lb
Tractive effort: 7,260lb

One of a number of Sentinel shunters introduced on to the LNER from 1927 onwards. Built in 1933 by the Sentinel Wagon Co, (works No 8837) it was at first LNER No 59, renumbered 8153 in 1946, then British Railways No 68153, later transferred to Departmental Stock as No 54. Withdrawn in 1961 and purchased by the Middleton Railway Preservation Society, it is to be seen at their premises at Leeds, restored to Departmental No 54. A similar engine, No 6515 of 1926, originally GWR No 12, later sold to Isebrook Quarry, Burton Latimer, Northants, became No 2

Isebrook and is now to be seen at Quainton Road.

Ravenglass & Eskdale Railway 0–8–2 1927

Driving wheels: 1ft 5½in
Cylinders: 5½in×8in
Gauge: 1ft 3in

Actually a rebuild of the original Duffield Bank 0–8–0T *Muriel* built in 1894, but the transfor-mation being so complete it is more appropriate to list it chronologically as having been built in 1927, the date of the conversion. It is now No 3 *River Irt*. The Ravenglass & Eskdale Railway, an old line originally opened in 1875 and closed in 1912, was reopened in 1915 by

the newly formed Eskdale Railway, since taken over and operated by the Ravenglass & Eskdale Railway Preservation Society.

LNER Gresley Class D49 4–4–0 No 246 'Morayshire'

1927

Driving wheels: 6ft 8in
Weight: 66 tons
Cylinders: (3) 17in×26in
Pressure: 180lb
Tractive effort: 21,555lb

Gresley's three-cylinder 'Shire' Class D49. Built at Darlington in 1927, it became No 2712 in 1946 and British Railways No 62712 in 1948. Withdrawn from service in 1961 and acquired

by I. N. Fraser of Arbroath for preservation. Restored to LNER livery – not the original style which was in use when the engine was built with the number on the tender, but the modified 1928 pattern in which the number appears on the cabside. It took part in the 150th Anniversary procession at Shildon in August 1975, and is now housed at the premises of the Scottish Preservation Society at Falkirk.

SR Class U 2–6–0

1928

Driving wheels: 6ft 0in
Cylinders: 19in×28in
Pressure: 200lb
Tractive effort: 23,865lb

The origin of this class lies in the ill-fated 'River' 2–6–4Ts of which the original appeared on the SE&CR in 1917, followed by 19 more built by the SR in 1925/6. After the disastrous Sevenoaks accident in 1927 they were all rebuilt as 2–6–0 tender engines, and another

thirty followed new in this form in 1928-1931. No 31618 was one of these, appearing from Brighton in 1928 as SR No A618, later No 1618, and finally BR No 31618. Withdrawn from service in January 1964 it has been re-prieved from Barry scrapyard by the Southern Mogul Preservation Society. The engine is on the Bluebell Railway, repainted in early SR livery; No 31806 and No 31625 have been acquired by the Mid-Hants Railway and No 31638 is a further candidate for preservation.

GWR 'Hall' Class 4—6—0

1928

Driving wheels: 6ft 0in
Weight: 75 tons
Cylinders: 18½in × 30in
Pressure: 225lb
Tractive effort: 27,275lb

Collett's well known standard mixed traffic design for the Great Western Railway, 330 of these engines were built. Withdrawn from service in 1965, one of the last to remain in traffic, No 6998 *Burton Agnes Hall* (built in 1949) has together with No 5900 *Hinderton Hall* been acquired by the Great Western Society and these two are now at Didcot. No 6960 *Raveningham Hall* on the Severn Valley Railway along with No 4930 *Hagley Hall*, No 4983 *Albert Hall* is at Tyseley. No 4920 *Dumbleton Hall* is on the Dart Valley Railway, No 6989 *Wightwick Hall* is at Quainton Road and is to be joined by No 4979 *Wootton Hall*.

No 6990 *Witherslack Hall* is on the GCR Main Line Steam Trust of Loughborough. Yet another rescue from Barry scrapyard is No 4942 *Maindy Hall* also secured by the Great Western Railway Society and brought to Didcot. The Society has plans to rebuild this engine as a 'Saint' of which historic class the last example, No 2920 *Saint David*, was regrettably cut up in 1953 just before the preservation movement really got under way. This ambitious project would be a reverse process of that which took place in 1924, when No 2925 *Saint Martin* was reconstructed and as No 4900 became the prototype of the numerous 'Hall' class to be constructed in large numbers over the ensuing years. The main alteration would be the substitution of 6ft 8½in driving wheels for the 6ft 0in size of the 'Halls'. Nos 6989, 6990 and 6998 are a development of the 'Hall' class and are known as 'Modified Halls'.

GWR Class 57xx 0–6–0PT 1929

Driving wheels: 4ft 7½in
Weight: 47½ tons
Cylinders: 17½in × 24in
Pressure: 200lb
Tractive effort: 22,515lb

Representative of the standard 'all purpose' pannier tanks introduced by the GWR in 1929 for replacement of many classes of older but very similar engines. In all there were no fewer than 863 engines, almost the largest class total ever known in this country, exceeded only by the 943 DX goods built at Crewe, of which no specimen survives. No 9642, built at Swindon in 1946, was the first to be preserved, by the 9642 Preservation Group at Maesteg, Glam. Nos 3650 and 3738 are preserved at the Didcot Ralway Centre, and Nos 5764 and 7714

on the Severn Valley Railway. No 9600 has been acquired by the Tyseley Steam Centre. No 9681 at the Norchard Steam Centre, with headquarters at Norchard near Lydney. No 3612 has gone to the Severn Valley as a source of spares. A number of these engines were sold at varying times between 1956 and 1963 to the London Transport Board for use on works trains and departmental duties, and some of these remained in service as late as 1971, three years after the cessation of steam working on BR. These were all of the earlier series with slightly smaller cabs than the later ones.

Several of these have been acquired by preservation societies:

LT No	GWR No	Built	New owners and location
L89	5775	1929	K&WVR, Haworth
L90	7760	1930	Tyseley Steam Centre
L92	5786	1930	Worcester Loco Society (At Bulmer's, Hereford)
L94	7752	1930	Tyseley Steam Centre
L95	5764	1929	Severn Valley Railway, Bridgnorth
L99	7715	1930	Quainton Road

Styles of restoration vary, some have been painted in GWR style, either green or black but No L89, is in London Transport maroon as illustrated.

SR 'Schools' Class 4–4–0 1930

Driving wheels: 6ft 7in
Weight: 67 tons 2 cwt
Cylinders: (3) 16½in × 26in
Pressure: 220lb
Tractive effort: 25,135lb

Probably Maunsell's most successful design, and certainly among the finest 4–4–0 engines ever constructed. Between 1930 and 1935 40 engines were built, and gave many years of excellent service on the SE&CR main lines, and also on the Western section to Portsmouth and Bournemouth. Three of them have been preserved, all were built at Eastleigh in 1934, and withdrawn in 1962. No 926 *Repton* went to the USA but now works on the Cape Breton Steam Railway in Canada. No 928 *Stowe* is on the East Somerset Railway at Cranmore and No 30925 (BR) *Cheltenham* is part of the National Railway Museum collection.

GWR Class 2251 0–6–0 No 3205 1930

Driving wheels: 5ft 2in
Weight: 43 tons 8 cwt
Cylinders: 17½in × 24in
Pressure: 200lb
Tractive effort: 20,155lb

Collett's 1930 design of 0–6–0 for the GWR. No 3205 was built in 1946 and withdrawn in 1965. It has been acquired privately for preservation, and now works on the Severn Valley Railway.

CDR 0–4–0 steam/diesel shunter No 11 'Phoenix' 1932

Weight: 12 tons
Engine: Gardner 6L2 diesel 74bhp

Originally built by Atkinson Walker in 1929 (works No 114) as a steam shunter for the Clogher Valley Railway. Sold in 1932 to the County Donegal and rebuilt as a diesel locomotive, becoming their No 11 *Phoenix*. It was withdrawn on the closure of the line in 1959, and is now in Belfast Museum.

GNR(I) 4–4–0 No 85 'Merlin' 1932

Driving wheels: 6ft 7in
Weight: (including tender) 103 tons 11 cwt
Cylinders: (1 high pressure inside 17¾in × 26in) (2 low pressure outside 19in × 26in)
Pressure: 250lb (later reduced to 215lb)
Tractive effort: 23,760lb (20,435lb) (superheated)
Gauge: 5ft 3in

Designed by G. T. Glover, and one of five engines constructed in 1932 for working the accelerated Dublin to Belfast expresses. They were built with round-topped boilers, but rebuilt with Belpaires in 1950, with reduced boiler pressure. It was the last new compound design in the British Isles, and one of the last 4–4–0 types. No 85 *Merlin* was Beyer Peacock works No 6733 of 1932. Originally turned out

in black, they later received the striking blue livery with red underframes introduced by the GNR after the war, and it was in this state that the engine was preserved in Belfast Museum, after having been withdrawn in 1961, the last of its class. It has now passed to the care of the RPSI and is being restored for main line running.

GWR Class 14xx 0–4–2T   1932

Driving wheels: 5ft 2in
Weight: 41 tons 6 cwt
Cylinders: 16in × 24in
Pressure: 165lb
Tractive effort: 13,900lb

Between 1932 and 1936 95 new engines of this class were built to replace similar but very much older locomotives, dating back to the 19th century, on branch line work. Most of them were fitted with pull and push apparatus. Four of them have been preserved, three in working order, Nos 1420 and 1450 on the

Dart Valley Railway, and No 1466 by the Great Western Society at Didcot Railway Centre; another, No 1442, is a static exhibit in Tiverton Museum. The engines were originally Nos 4820, 4850, 4866 and 4842, assuming their present numbers in 1946. Brief history and particulars are as follows:

No	Built	Withdrawn
1420	1933	1964
1442	1935	1965
1450	1935	1965
1466	1936	1963

GWR Class 64xx 0–6–0PT   1932

Driving wheels: 4ft 7½in
Weight: 45 tons 12 cwt
Cylinders: 16½in × 24in

Pressure: 165lb
Tractive effort: 16,510lb

Between 1932 and 1937 40 engines were built, being one of the many varieties of the well known pannier tanks used in large numbers all over the Great Western system for so many years. They were fitted with pull and push apparatus for motor working. Three were acquired by the Dart Valley Railway. They are numbers 6412, 6430 and 6435, built at Swindon, the first in 1934 and the others in 1937, and withdrawn by British Railways in 1964. No 6412 has since been sold to the West Somerset Railway where it now carries the name *The Flockton Flyer* following its role in the children's TV series.

LMS 0–6–0 diesel shunter 1932

Driving wheels: 3ft 0in
Weight: 21½ tons
Tractive effort: 10,520lb

Built by the Hunslet Engine Co in 1932 (works No 1697), it was one of the first diesel locomotives in the country; being one of several experimental shunting engines obtained by the LMS at this period, which were the forerunners of the standard diesel-electric locomotives now so commonly in use. This particular engine was a diesel mechanical 0–6–0 and now has a 132hp Maclaren/Ricardo engine. Originally LMS No 7401, it was transferred to the War Department as WD No 27 in 1940, later returning to the LMS as No 7051, being withdrawn from service in 1945, and returned to the makers who repaired it and loaned it for industrial use. Purchased by the Middleton Railway Preservation Society in 1960 and named *John Alcock*. At present on loan to the National Railway Museum, York.

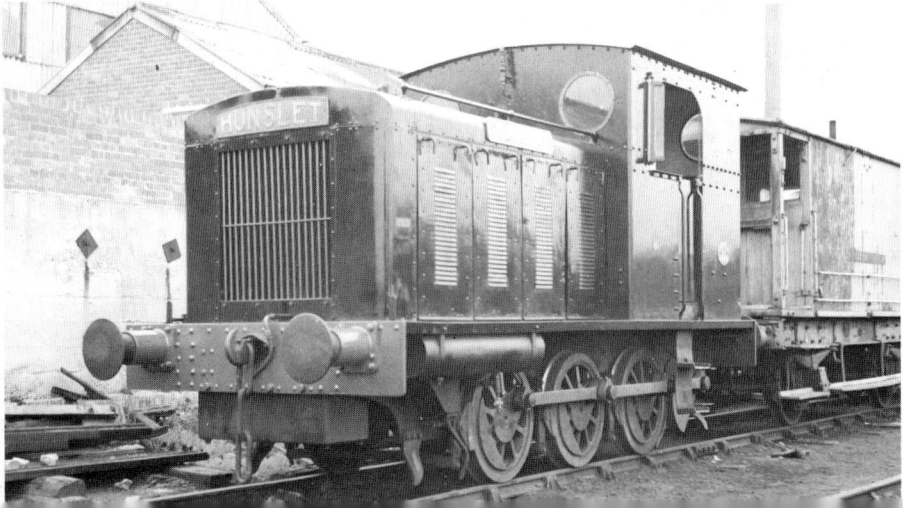

LMS Stanier Class 7P 4–6–2 1933

Driving wheels: 6ft 6in
Weight: (engine only) 104½ tons
Cylinders: (4) 16½in × 28in
Pressure: 250lb
Tractive effort: 40,285lb

Stanier's original Pacific design, introduced in 1933, of which 12 examples were built. Two have been preserved privately, both restored to LMS livery. No 6203 *Princess Margaret*

Rose, for many years at Butlin's Holiday Camp, Pwllheli, was recently acquired by the Midland Railway Trust, Butterley; and No 6201 *Princess Elizabeth*, owned by the Princess Elizabeth Loco Society, is now accommodated by Bulmer's, Hereford. It took part in the 150th Anniversary procession at Shildon in August 1975, and has since worked some specials over authorised BR routes.

LMS Stanier Class 5MT 2–6–0 No 42968 1933

Driving wheels: 5ft 6in
Weight: (engine only) 69 tons 2 cwt
Cylinders: 18in × 28in
Pressure: 225lb
Tractive effort: 26,290lb

One of Sir William Stanier's first designs after coming over to the LMS from the GWR in 1932. Forty engines were built in 1933 and 1934, Nos 13245-13284, later Nos 2945-2984, eventually BR Nos 42945-42984. The last survivor, No 42968, has been rescued from Barry scrapyard by the Severn Valley Railway.

GWR Class 72xx 2–8–2T No 7202 1934

Driving wheels: 4ft 7½in
Weight: 92½ tons
Cylinders: 19in×30in
Pressure: 200lb
Tractive effort: 33,170lb

The 54 engines of this class, Nos 7200-7253, were all conversions from 2–8–0Ts, a Churchward design, which had been built between 1910 and 1930. The reconstructions took place from 1934 to 1939, and were the result of the depression of the 1930s which made many of them temporarily redundant on the short hauls in the South Valley coalfields, for which they had been designed. As rebuilt with increased coal and water capacity they could be transferred to more main line duties. No 7202, to be seen at the Didcot Railway Centre, was built as 2–8–0 No 5277 in 1930 and converted to 2–8–2T in 1934. The Quainton Railway Society are planning to acquire No 7200 from Barry Scrapyard.

LMS Stanier Class 5MT 4–6–0   1934

Driving wheels: 6ft 0in
Weight: 72 tons 2 cwt
Cylinders: 18½in×28in
Pressure: 225lb
Tractive effort: 25,455lb

One of the most versatile and generally useful designs of locomotive ever produced in this country. It was almost the last class to remain in any appreciable numbers on BR until the end of steam, and it is not surprising therefore that although no specimen had been acquired for preservation up to 1967 when the first edition of this book was produced, there are now no fewer than 12. In all 842 were built (some with sundry modifications, such as Caprotti valve gear) between 1934 and 1950, numbered 44658-45499, and the design formed the basis of the subsequent BR Standard 73000 class (see page 118). The following have been preserved:

44806 Now named *Magpie*: worked for a time on the Lakeside & Haverthwaite Railway, but is now at Steamport, Southport.

44871 At Steamtown, Carnforth, to remain in BR livery, named *Sovereign*.
44932 At Steamtown, Carnforth, painted in BR Brunswick green.
5000 Part of the National Railway Museum Collection. On loan to the Severn Valley Railway.
5025 Restored as LMS No 5025, on Strathspey Railway.
45110 Purchased by the Stanier Black 5 Preservation Society, named *RAF Biggin Hill* and now working on the Severn Valley Railway.
45212 Purchased by Ron Ainsworth for use on the Keighley & Worth Valley Railway.
5231 In LMS livery– GCR Main Line Steam Trust, Loughborough.
5305 Purchased by Albert Draper, Scrapbreaker, Hull. Restored to working order by Humberside Locomotive Preservation Society. On loan to National Railway Museum, York.
45379 Bristol Industrial Museum, Princes Wharf, Bristol.
45407 At Steamtown, Carnforth.

5428 Preserved by Stanier Black 5 Preservation Society. Named *Eric Treacy*. Now on the North Yorkshire Moors Railway.

Amongst the variations of the 'Black Fives', No 44767 was unique in that it was fitted with Stephenson's valve gear instead of the usual Walschaerts. (Twenty of them, Nos 44738 to 44757, had Caprotti valve gear, but none of these has survived.) It was built at Crewe in 1947 as LMS No 4767, and like two or three

other 'Black Fives', was also unusual in having a double chimney, later replaced by a single chimney. It spent most of its time in the north, and was rarely seen in London, although it did appear on odd occasions. Latterly it was stationed at Bank Hall, and finally at Carlisle (Kingmoor). It was purchased by Brian Hollingsworth on withdrawal in 1967. After a sojourn at Steamtown, Carnforth, it is now on the North Yorkshire Moors Railway, named *George Stephenson*.

LMS Class 4P 2–6–4T No 2500   1934

Driving wheels: 5ft 9in
Weight: 92¼ tons
Cylinders: (3) 16in×26in

Pressure: 200lb
Tractive effort: 24,600lb

A three-cylinder version of Stanier's express passenger tank design, 37 engines of which were built for use on the London, Tilbury and Southend section in 1934, No 2500 being the first, it became LMS No 42500. All were with-drawn in 1961 and 1962 when the LT&SR was electrified, but No 42500 has been preserved. Now at Bressingham Hall, Diss, Norfolk, as illustrated, restored as LMS No 2500.

LMS 'Jubilee' class 4–6–0   1934

Driving wheels: 6ft 9in
Weight: 79 tons 11 cwt
Cylinders: (3) 17in×26in
Pressure: 225lb
Tractive effort: 26,610lb

One of the last of Sir William Stanier's express design of 1934 to remain in traffic. No 45596 *Bahamas* was acquired in 1967 for preservation by the Bahamas Locomotive Society, Dinting, where it was joined by No 45690

Leander. This locomotive, restored to LMS maroon livery, has worked a number of main line railtours. It moved to Carnforth in 1979. Another engine, No 45593, *Kolhapur* has been acquired by the Standard Gauge Steam Trust and can be seen at Tyseley on Open Days. All restored to LMS maroon livery with old numbers, 5596, 5690 and 5593. No 45699 *Galatea* has been purchased from Barry as a source of spares for No 5690 but may be restored to working order.

GWR Class 1366 0–6–0PT No 1369   1934

Driving wheels: 3ft 8in
Weight: 35¾ tons
Cylinders: 16in×20in
Pressure: 165lb
Tractive effort: 16,320lb

One of a class of six engines built at Swindon in 1934. Amongst other duties, an important one for many years was the hauling of the Channel Islands boat trains through the streets of Weymouth between the station and the

quayside. In their last years three of them, including No 1369, took over the working of the LSWR Wenford Bridge mineral line in North Cornwall from the Beattie 2–4–0Ts (see page 27) but this was very short-lived, and they were replaced by diesels in 1964. No 1369 is now the property of the Dart Valley Railway and the illustration shows it at Buckfastleigh in 1971.

LNER Gresley Class A4 4–6–2   1935

Driving wheels: 6ft 8in
Weight: (engine only) 102 tons 19 cwt
Cylinders: (3) 18½in × 26in
Pressure: 250lb
Tractive effort: 34,555lb

Sir Nigel Gresley's revolutionary streamlined design of 1935, originally introduced for working the 'Silver Jubilee' high speed trains between London and Newcastle, to be followed by other similar services. The most famous of the class was undoubtedly *Mallard*

which attained a world record, fully authenticated, for steam traction of 126mile/h on a test run on 3 July 1938 down Stoke Bank. *Mallard* was built in 1938 as LNER No 4468, subsequently becoming No 22 in 1946, upon Nationalisation at first BR No E22 and later No 60022. It was in the Museum of British Transport at Clapham until the latter's closure in 1973, after which it was removed to York, restored to its original condition (except for absence of corridor tender) in blue livery. The only substantial alteration it had undergone

was the removal of the side valances over the coupling rods, but these were replaced when the engine was restored. This has not been done in the case of the other engines of the class which have been resuscitated. The six preserved examples are:

Nos 4468 and 4498 are in LNER blue livery, but the others are in their final BR condition, except for *Bittern*, which carries its 1946 number, 19. Nos 4498 and 60009 are in working order.

Original No	Later No	BR No	Name	Preserved by
4468	22	60022	*Mallard*	National Railway Museum, York
4498	7	60007	*Sir Nigel Gresley*	A4 Preservation Society, Steamtown, Carnforth
4496	8	60008	*Dwight D. Eisenhower*	National Railway Museum, Wisconsin, USA
4488	9	60009	*Union of South Africa*	Markinch, Fife
4489	10	60010	*Dominion of Canada*	Canadian Railroad Historical Association, Delson, Montreal
4464	19	60019	*Bittern*	Privately preserved at Dinting Railway Centre

LMS Stanier Class 8F 2–8–0

1935

Driving wheels: 4ft 8½in
Weight: 72 tons 2 cwt
Cylinders: 18½in × 28in
Pressure: 225lb
Tractive effort: 32,440lb

Stanier's standard freight engine, of which several hundred were built between 1935 and 1946. No 48773 was built by the NB Loco Co in 1940 (works No 24607) as LMSR No 8233, being transferred to the War Department in 1941 as WD No 307 and sent overseas, where it became Iran State Railway Nos 41-109. Returned to this country as WD No 70307 in 1952, it was repaired at Derby as WD No 500 and sent to Longmoor, but in June 1957 it was at Bicester. Reabsorbed into BR stock the same year, at first allocated the number 90733 in error following the Austerity 2–8–0s with which it was confused, but quickly altered to No 48773, at the end of the LMS 2–8–0s. Withdrawn 1968 and acquired by the Stanier 8F Locomotive Society. Restored as LMS No 8233, it works on the Severn Valley Railway.

Another one, No 8431 built at Swindon in 1944, is on the Keighley & Worth Valley Railway, while No 48151 is at Embsay, Yorkshire Dales Railway.

LNER Gresley Class V2 2–6–2 No 4771 'Green Arrow'

1936

Driving wheels: 6ft 2in
Weight: 93 tons 2 cwt
Cylinders: (3) 18½in × 26in
Pressure: 220lb
Tractive effort: 33,730lb

Sir Nigel Gresley's mixed traffic design of 1936. In all, 184 engines were constructed, and they did yeoman service for many years on the old Great Northern Main line (and in Scotland), particularly during the 1940s, since when they have sometimes been described

as 'the engines which won the war'. The original No 4771 *Green Arrow* was initially allocated the number 700 under the 1944 re-numbering scheme, which was however, only put into effect in a few instances and later amended, under which it actually became No 800 in 1946. Becoming BR No 60800, it was withdrawn from service in 1962, and repainted in original LNER condition. Now restored to working order and used on steam specials, it is normally housed in the National Railway Museum, York. It took part in the 150th Anniversary procession at Shildon in August 1975.

GWR Class 90xx 4–4–0 No 3217   1936

Driving wheels: 5ft 8in
Weight: 49 tons
Cylinders: 18in × 26in
Pressure: 180lb
Tractive effort: 18,955lb

Although nominally a new engine built at Swindon in 1938, this was actually a reconstruction of two locomotives, embodying parts of one of Dean's 'Duke of Cornwall' class engines built in 1895, No 3258 *The Lizard*, together with the frames of one of the later 'Bulldog' class, No 3425 built in 1906. In all 28 pairs of engines were dealt with in this way, between 1936 and 1939 and the resulting 'new' productions soon earned themselves the nickname of 'Dukedogs' for obvious reasons. It was renumbered 9017 in 1946, and on withdrawal in 1960 was acquired by the Bluebell Railway, and is now to be seen at Sheffield Park. When the 'Castle' engine *Earl of Berkeley* was withdrawn in 1963, its name-plates were secured and placed on the 4–4–0, as had been the original intention, and at the same time it received its old number 3217, these plates again being obtained from the Collett 0–6–0 which had taken its number.

LNER Class K4 2–6–0 No 3442 'The Great Marquess'   1937

Driving wheels: 5ft 2in
Weight: 68 tons 8 cwt
Cylinders: (3) 18½in × 26in
Pressure: 200lb
Tractive effort: 36,600lb

Gresley's specially designed 2–6–0 for the West Highland Line, six of which were built in 1937 and 1938. No 3442 *The Great Marquess* was renumbered 1994 in 1946, and became BR 61994. Withdrawn from service in 1961, it was acquired by Lord Garnock and restored to LNER livery in working order. It is now on the Severn Valley Railway.

LMS Stanier Class 8P 4–6–2   1937

Driving wheels: 6ft 9in
Weight: 105 tons 5 cwt (108 tons 2 cwt in streamlined condition)
Cylinders: (4) 16¼in×28in
Pressure: 250lb
Tractive effort: 40,000lb

Sir William Stanier's later Pacific design; 38 engines were built between 1937 and 1948, of which Nos 6220-6229 and 6235-6248 were turned out with streamlined casings (subsequently removed) and Nos 6230-6234 and 6249-6257 without streamlining. Three of these engines have been preserved. No 6229

Duchess of Hamilton was being restored to working order for operation in 1980 from the National Railway Museum, York. No 6233 *Duchess of Sutherland* is at Bressingham Hall. Both are in LMS livery. No 6229 was, incidentally, the engine that went to the USA in 1938, masquerading as No 6220 *Coronation*. No 46235 (BR number) *City of Birmingham* is preserved in the Birmingham Museum of Science and Industry, but not in its original condition, as it was one of the streamlined series. The illustration shows No 6233 at Bressingham Hall in 1974.

GWR 'Manor' Class 4–6–0   1938

Driving wheels: 5ft 8in
Weight: 68 tons 18 cwt
Cylinders: 18in×30in
Pressure: 225lb
Tractive effort: 27,340lb

Collett's 4–6–0 design of 1938 for use over lines with weight restrictions precluding the use of heavier engines, notably the former Cambrian and the Midland and South Western Junction Railways. No 7808 *Cookham Manor* spent its working life over both routes. It ran

until 1965 and is now at Didcot Railway Centre. No 7827 *Lydham Manor* is on the Dart Valley Railway, No 7812 *Erlestoke Manor* and No 7819 *Hinton Manor* on the Severn Valley Railway. No 7822 *Foxcote Manor* is with the Cambrian Railways Society at Oswestry. No 7820 *Dinmore Manor* is on the Gwili Railway in Wales.

SR Maunsell Class Q 0–6–0 No 30541   1938

Driving wheels: 5ft 1in
Weight: 49½ tons
Cylinders: 19in×26in
Pressure: 200lb
Tractive effort: 26,160lb

Maunsell's general purpose 0–6–0, introduced in 1938, of which 20, Nos 530 to 549 (later BR Nos 30530 to 30549), were built. The last survivor, BR No 30541, has been acquired from Barry scrapyard by the Maunsell Q Locomotive Preservation Society. It spent some years undergoing restoration at the Dowty Preservation Society's premises in Ashchurch; it was transferred to the Bluebell Railway in 1978. Photographed at Bournemouth shed in 1960.

GSR(I) 4–6–0 No 800 'Maeve'   1939

Driving wheels: 6ft 7in
Weight: 84 tons
Cylinders: (3) 18½in×28in
Pressure: 225lb
Tractive effort: 33,000lb
Gauge: 5ft 3in

One of three engines built in 1939 for working the heaviest expresses between Dublin and Cork. They were named after Queens of Ireland, Nos 800 *Maeve*, 801 *Macha* and 802 *Tailte*, and they were destined to be the last new conventional steam locomotives con-

structed for the GSR(I), or Coras Iompair Eireann, as it later became. They were very similar
to the rebuilt 'Royal Scots' of the LMS, both in
appearance and dimensions. No 800 is now
preserved in Belfast Museum.

SR 'Merchant Navy' Class 4–6–2   1941

Driving wheels: 6ft 2in
Weight: 97 tons 18 cwt
Cylinders: (3) 18in×24in
Pressure: 250lb
Tractive effort: 33,495lb

Bulleid's first revolutionary design of Pacific
introduced in 1941. Originally streamlined,
with 280lb pressure and Bulleid's chain driven
valve gear. The whole class was later modified
with Walschaerts valve gear and other details,
and the air-smoothed casing removed, No
35028 *Clan Line* (originally built in 1948) being
thus treated in November 1959. Withdrawn in
July 1967 on completion of the Bournemouth
electrification, together with all the other remaining SR steam locomotives. It has been
acquired by the Merchant Navy Locomotive
Preservation Society, and is now at Bulmer's,
Hereford. Frequently in steam on special on
approved BR lines. Another of the class No
35005, *Canadian Pacific* is at Steamtown,
Carnforth, undergoing restoration, No 35018
British India Line is on the Mid-Hants Railway,
and No 35029 is on display in York Museum,
sectionalised to show its interior working
parts.

LNER Thompson Class B1 4–6–0 1942

Driving wheels: 6ft 2in
Weight: 71 tons 3 cwt
Cylinders: 20×26in
Pressure: 225lb
Tractive effort: 26,880lb

Thompson's general purpose mixed traffic engine introduced in 1942 to replace ageing LNER engines, notably the Atlantics of the GNR, GCR and NER, and other elderly 4–4–0s and 4–6–0s. The first 41 carried names of South African fauna, becoming known as the 'Antelope' class. The numbers were Nos 1000-1009 (originally 8301-8310) 1010-1287, BR Nos E1288-E1303 and Nos 61304-61400. No 61306 carries works plates NB Loco Co works No 26157 of 1947, although it did not appear until early in 1948, and was one of the first to carry a BR number from the start. Now restored by the B1 Locomotive Society in LNER green livery as No 1306 *Mayflower*, it is now with the GCR Main Line Steam Trust, Loughborough, who also accommodate No 61264, the only other member of the class to have survived.

SR Bulleid Class Q1 0–6–0 No 33001 1942

Driving wheels: 5ft 1in
Weight: 51¼ tons
Cylinders: 19in×26in
Pressure: 230lb
Tractive effort: 30,080lb

Produced under conditions of wartime austerity in 1942, these unconventional engines earned for themselves the dubious distinction of being amongst the ugliest ever designed. They were, notwithstanding, most efficient machines, and achieved their object in attaining maximum power with minimum weight. Forty of them were built at Brighton and Ashford works, and the initial engine No C1 (later BR No 33001), withdrawn in 1964, was retained for preservation and is at present on loan to the Bluebell Railway.

SR Class USA 0–6–0T

1942

Driving wheels: 4ft 6in
Weight: 46½ tons
Cylinders: 16½in × 24in
Pressure: 210lb
Tractive effort: 21,600lb

One of a large number of powerful shunting tank engines built in the USA for war service in this country and overseas. This particular one was built in 1943 by the Vulcan Ironworks USA (works No 4432), not to be confused with the Vulcan Foundry in this country. In October 1945 it was in store at Newbury along with 30 others of the class. Eventually 14 of these engines were purchased by the Southern Railway for use in Southampton docks. It became SR No 64 and later BR No 30064. Acquired by the Southern Locomotive Preservation Society it is now on the Bluebell Railway. Three others of the class have been preserved No 30072, by the Keighley & Worth Valley Railway, and two others latterly in use as works shunters at Ashford, Nos DS237 *Wainwright* and DS238 *Maunsell*. These have been acquired by the Kent & East Sussex Railway and are now K&ESR Nos 21 and 22. They were formerly BR Nos 30065 and 30070.

War Department Austerity 2–8–0

1943

Driving wheels: 4ft 8½in
Weight (loco only): 70¼ tons
Cylinders: 19in × 28in
Pressure: 225lb
Tractive effort: 34,215lb

A War Department design introduced in 1943 for use both at home and overseas. Many hundreds were built, and no fewer than 733 of them eventually came into the hands of British Railways, numbered 90000-90732. Somewhat remarkably, none of these survived the holocaust of the 1950s and 1960s, but one which went abroad has been rescued by the Keighley & Worth Railway Valley. Built by the Vulcan Foundry in 1945 as WD No 79257, it went to Holland and became Dutch State No 4464, was sold in 1952 to the Swedish State as their No 1931, and is now to be seen at Haworth on the K&WVR.

War Department Austerity 2–10–0

1943

Driving wheels: 4ft 8½in
Weight: 78½ tons
Cylinders: 19in×28in

Pressure: 225lb
Tractive effort: 34,215lb

Designed by R. A. Riddles for use at home and overseas, 150 engines were built between 1943 and 1945. Originally WD No 3651, the second engine of the class, it was built by the North British Locomotive Co Ltd in 1943 (works No 25437), to be sent to the railway training centre at Longmoor. In 1944 it became No 73651, and in 1952 No 600, receiving the name *Gordon*. Acquired by the Transport Trust, it is now on the Severn Valley Railway at Bridgnorth. Another of the class, No 73755 *Longmoor* (NB Loco Co 1945, works No 25601) was purchased by the Netherlands Railways, with which it was in service until 1951; it is now in the Dutch Railway Museum at Utrecht.

SR 'Battle of Britain' Class 4–6–2

1945

Driving wheels: 6ft 2in
Weight: 86 tons
Cylinders: (3) 16⅜in×24in
Pressure: 250lb
Tractive effort: 27,715lb

Bulleid's lighter design of Pacific for the Southern Railway, introduced at the end of World War II, the first engines appearing in 1945. 110 engines were constructed, 60 of which were subsequently rebuilt on more conventional lines with Walschaerts valve gear (see page 124) and with the streamlining removed, but *Winston Churchill* was not one

of those so treated. Originally numbered 21C151, it became 34051 on Nationalisation, and lasted until September 1965, when it was scheduled by BR for preservation. It is now on loan to Didcot Railway Centre. One of its final duties was most appropriately to haul the train bearing the mortal remains of the Great Man after whom it was named, from Waterloo to Handborough, on 30 January 1965. No 21C123 *Blackmoor Vale* is on the Bluebell Railway, No 34092 *City of Wells* the K&WVR. No 34081 *92 Squadron* on the Nene Valley and No 34105 *Swanage* on the Mid-Hants, Alresford.

LMS Fairburn Class 4MT 2–6–4T

1945

Driving wheels: 5ft 9in
Weight: 85¼ tons
Cylinders: 19⅝in×26in
Pressure: 200lb
Tractive effort: 24,670lb

Fairburn's development of Stanier's 1935 design of express tank engine, of which 170 were built between 1945 and 1951. Two of the last survivors were Nos 42073 and 42085, built at Brighton in 1950 and 1951. At first they were allocated to the Southern Region, but in 1953 were transferred to the North Eastern, where they spent the rest of their working lives. Withdrawn in 1967, they have been purchased for use on the Lakeside Railway, Haverthwaite. They have been repainted as No 2073 in LNWR livery and No 2085 in Caledonian blue.

LMS Ivatt Class 2MT 2–6–0

1946

Driving wheels: 5ft 0in
Weight: 47 tons 2 cwt
Cylinders: 16in×24in
Pressure: 200lb
Tractive effort: 17,410lb

H. G. Ivatt's light engine design of 1946 for the LMS, Nos 6400-6419 were built at Crewe in 1946/7. The remainder were built after Nationalisation as Nos 46420-46527. The class was perpetuated in all essentials as the BR Standard 78000 class, which eventually totalled 65 further engines. (See page 121.) No 46464, built at Crewe in 1950 and the first to be preserved, is now on the Strathspey Railway. No 46512 is also to go to the Strathspey Railway, but at the time of writing it is in store at Hereford. No 46441, which has been repainted Midland red and given an LMS number, 6441, that, like its present livery, it never actually carried, may be seen

at Steamtown, Carnforth. No 46447, property of the Ivatt Trust, is at Quainton Road under restoration. Whilst Nos 6443 and 46521 are on the Severn Valley Railway. The remains of No 46428 in Barry Scrapyard have been purchased as spares for No 46464 by the Strathspey Railway.

LMS Ivatt Class 2MT 2–6–2T

Driving wheels: 5ft 0in
Weight: 63¼ tons

Cylinders: 16in×24in
Pressure: 200lb
Tractive effort: 17,410lb

Tank counterpart of the 2—6—0 just described, these engines were for light passenger and branch line work, some of them being motor fitted. Ten engines were built by the LMS in 1946, and another 120 by BR after Nationalisation. No 41241, withdrawn in 1966, was acquired privately for preservation, and is at Haworth, headquarters of the Keighley & Worth Valley Railway. Two others of the class, Nos 41298 and 41313, have been purchased by the Ivatt Locomotive Trust and are at Quainton Road, under restoration. No 41312 is preserved by the Caerphilly Railway Society at the old Rhymney Railway works at Caerphilly.

LMS(NCC) Class 4MT 2–6–4T No 4

Driving wheels: 6ft 0in
Weight: 87½ tons
Cylinders: 19in×26in
Pressure: 200lb
Tractive effort: 22,160lb
Gauge: 5ft 3in

A class of 18 engines built at Derby in 1946-1950 to the 5ft 3in gauge for service on the NCC in Ireland, where they were used on express duties from Belfast both to Larne and Londonderry. The complete series was numbered 1-10 and 50-57. Apart from the difference of gauge, they were largely based on the original LMS Fowler design of 1927, none of which has survived from BR. No 4, built in 1947, was one of the last survivors in 1970, and on withdrawal was acquired by the Railway Preservation Society of Ireland for use on rail tours, and it is periodically to be seen at work in both Northern and Southern Ireland.

LMS Ivatt Class 4MT 2–6–0 No 43106

Driving wheels: 5ft 3in
Weight: 59 tons 2 cwt
Cylinders: 17½in×26in
Pressure: 225lb
Tractive effort: 24,170lb

Introduced to the LMS by Ivatt just prior to Nationalisation (the first three engines actually came out in LMS livery), the class eventually totalled 162 engines. BR Nos 43000-43161. No 43106, built at Darlington in 1951, survived

until the end of steam in August, 1968, when it was rescued for use on the Severn Valley Railway. It took part in the 150th Anniversary procession at Shildon in August 1975.

GWR Class 94xx 0–6–0PT

1947

Driving wheels: 4ft 7½in
Weight: 55 tons 7 cwt
Cylinders: 17½in × 24in
Pressure: 200lb
Tractive effort: 22,515lb

Final development of the long line of GWR inside cylinder Saddle/Pannier Tanks, the complete history of which goes back to 1860. No 9400 was built at Swindon in 1947, a batch of 10 engines which were the last true Great Western engines, although some Great Western Railway types were perpetuated for two or three years after Nationalisation, including another 200 of the 9400 class, differing only from the original 10 in being unsuperheated. No 9400 itself was withdrawn from service in 1959 and is now preserved in Swindon Museum. No 9466 from Barry scrapyard has gone to Quainton Road.

GWR Hawksworth Class 15xx 0–6–0PT No 1501

1949

Driving wheels: 4ft 7½in
Weight: 58 tons 4 cwt
Cylinders: 17½in × 24in
Pressure: 200lb
Tractive effort: 22,515lb

Although essentially of Great Western design these engines did not in fact come out until after nationalisation, appearing in 1949. Only 10 were built, Nos 1500-1509, the last of a very long line, but differing considerably from their predecessors in having outside cylinders and Walschaerts valve gear. Most of them spent their short lives, consequent on dieselisation, on empty carriage stock workings between Paddington and Old Oak. Nos 1501, 1502 and 1509 were sold in 1961 to the NCB Coventry Colliery, and the first of these has been secured by the Severn Valley Railway, at Bridgnorth, the other two being cannibalised to provide spare parts. The illustration shows it at Southall in 1960.

LNER Peppercorn Class A2 4–6–2 No 532 'Blue Peter'

1947

Driving wheels: 6ft 2in
Weight: 101 tons
Cylinders: 19in × 26in
Pressure: 250lb
Tractive effort: 40,430lb

Peppercorn's version of Class A2, following Thompson's previous similar engines, but with a number of variations. No 60532 *Blue Peter* was built after Nationalisation in 1948, the first to come out under the new renum-

bering scheme. *Blue Peter* was the last survivor of 15 locomotives (Nos 60525-60539), withdrawn in 1966, and was acquired privately for preservation. It has been repainted as LNER No 532 although it just failed actually to appear as such in the first place. *Blue Peter* has, until recently, been in store with A4 Pacific *Bittern* but both locomotives are now at Dinting Railway Centre.

LNER Peppercorn Class K1 2–6–0 No 2005   1949

Driving wheels: 5ft 2in
Weight: 66 tons 17 cwt
Cylinders: 20in×26in
Pressure: 225lb
Tractive effort: 32,080lb

Essentially an LNER design, although it did not appear until after nationalisation. It was a direct development of Thompson's rebuild of Gresley K4 2–6–0 No 61997, converted from three to two cylinders in 1945. (No 3442 of Class K4 is also preserved, see page 104). Seventy engines, Nos 62001-62070, were built in 1949 and 1950. No 62005 was withdrawn in 1967. Purchased by Lord Garnock, J. B. Hollingsworth, G. Nissem and G. Drury. Presented to the North Eastern Locomotive Preservation Group. It has now been restored to working order on the North Yorkshire Moors Railway in LNER apple green livery as No 2005, although it never ran thus painted in ordinary service.

GWR Class 16xx 0–6–0PT No 1638   1949

Driving wheels: 4ft 1½in
Weight: 41 tons 12 cwt
Cylinders: 16½in × 24in
Pressure: 165lb
Tractive effort: 18,515lb

The last variety of earlier GWR pannier tank to appear. Although not actually built until after Nationalisation, they were of course a pure Great Western Railway design. Between 1949 and 1955 70 engines were constructed. Owing to the onset of dieselisation they had an exceptionally short life, and No 1638, built in 1951 and withdrawn in 1966, was one of the last survivors. It has been acquired by the Dart Valley Railway.

Sligo Leitrim & Northern Counties Railway 0–6–4T
1949

Driving wheels: 4ft 8in
Weight: 54½ tons
Cylinders: 18in × 24in
Pressure: 160lb
Gauge: 5ft 3in

Notable as being the last new conventional steam locomotive delivered to an Irish railway. It was one of a pair built by Messrs Beyer Peacock in 1949, this one, *Lough Erne*, being works No 7242. Owing to difficulties over payment, they did not arrive on the Sligo Leitrim & Northern Counties Railway until 1951, under a hire purchase agreement. On the closure of the line in 1957 they were sold by the makers to the Ulster Transport Authority and used for some years shunting at Belfast, this engine becoming UTA No 27. It has now been acquired by the Railway Preservation Society of Ireland. Seen here at Belfast, York Road in 1965.

BR Class 11 0–6–0 shunter
1950

Engine: English Electric 6-cyl
Weight: 47 tons
Tractive effort: 35,000lb
Transmission: Electric. Two nose suspended, double reduction gear drive

No 12077 was built at Derby in 1950, to an LMS design, and withdrawn from service at Wigan depot in October 1971. It remained in a scrap dealer's yard in Birmingham until December 1978 when it was purchased by the Midland Railway Trust and transported to their premises at Butterley.

BR Class 76 electric Bo-Bo

1950

Weight: 88 ton
Wheel diameter: 4ft 2in
Maximum tractive effort: 45,000lb

A class of 57 locomotives of LNER design, built in 1950 for the Manchester-Sheffield electrification scheme. Originally Nos 26001-26057, they were later known as Class 76 and became Nos 76.001-76.057. Owing to the decrease in traffic (now confined to freight) over this route some of them have been withdrawn. No 76.020 has gone to the National Railway Museum at York, restored to its original black livery and number.

BR 'Britannia' Class 4–6–2

1951

Driving wheels: 6ft 2in
Weight: 94 tons 4 cwt
Cylinders: 20in × 28in
Pressure: 250lb
Tractive effort: 32,150lb

The first of the 12 standard designs introduced by British Railways in 1951, all of which were intended to be constructed in large numbers, but which ambitious programme was ruthlessly brought to a halt when the decision to

abandon steam was suddenly made a few years later. Fifty-five 'Britannias' were constructed and proved themselves to be most excellent and efficient engines. No 70000 itself was withdrawn from service in 1966 and has been acquired by the Britannia Locomotive Society. It is now on the Severn Valley Railway. A second engine No 70013 *Oliver Cromwell*, the last locomotive to receive a general overhaul by BR, ran until the end of steam in August 1968, hauling many enthusiasts' specials. It has found a final resting place at Bressingham Hall, Diss, Norfolk.

BR Class 4MT 4–6–0 1951

Driving wheels: 5ft 8in
Weight: 69 tons
Cylinders: 18in × 28in
Pressure: 225lb
Tractive effort: 25,100lb

BR standard lightweight 4–6–0 design for cross-country and semi-main line work. 80 engines, Nos 75000-75079 were built between 1951 and 1956. It was one of the last BR classes to remain in traffic. No 75027 has been acquired by the Bluebell Railway, No 75029 by the East Somerset Railway, Cranmore, now named *The Green Knight*, No 75078 by the Keighley & Worth Valley Railway and No 75069 by the Severn Valley Railway. All except No 75027 carry double chimneys.

BR Class 5MT 4–6–0 1951

Driving wheels: 6ft 2in
Weight: 76¼ tons
Cylinders: 19in × 28in
Pressure: 225lb
Tractive effort: 26,120lb

BR's standard mixed traffic engine, developed from Stanier's LMS design of 1934. 172 engines, Nos 73000-73171, built between 1951 and 1957. Thirty of the engines were fitted with Caprotti valve gear (qv). No 73050 was turned out from Derby in 1954, and exhibited when new at Willesden Exhibition in that year. Withdrawn in 1968 when one of the last survivors, No 73050 was purchased by the Rev R.

Paton of Peterborough. Now named *City of Peterborough* it is in use on the Nene Valley Railway near Peterborough. No 73082 *Camelot* is on the Bluebell Railway.

BR Class 4MT 2–6–4T   1951

Driving wheels: 5ft 8in
Weight: 88½ tons
Cylinders: 18in × 28in
Pressure: 225lb
Tractive effort: 25,100lb

British Railways standard express tank engine design, a direct development from the corresponding LMS type; 155 were built between 1951 and 1957. Several have been acquired for preservation. No 80002 (illustrated prior to

preservation) is on the Keighley & Worth Valley Railway; No 80064 has been acquired by the Dart Valley Railway; No 80078 is undergoing restoration at Swanage; No 80079 is on the Severn Valley Railway; No 80100 is on the Bluebell Railway; No 80105 by the Scottish Railway Preservation Society at Falkirk; No 80135 by the North Yorkshire Moors Railway; No 80136 is at Cheedleton, North Staffordshire Railway Society, and No 80151 at the Chappel Steam Centre.

BR Drewry Class 04 0–6–0 shunter   1952

Wheel diameter: 3ft 3in (3ft 6in)
Weight: 29¼ tons (32 tons)
Engine: Gardner 204hp
Tractive effort: 16,850lb (15,650lb)

A class of shunting locomotives introduced in 1952, slightly modified in 1955. No D2271 was withdrawn from service in October 1969, it was sold out of service and eventually purchased by Mr S. G. Hibbert in 1972. It is now with the Midland Railway Trust at Butterley. Nos D2245 and D2298 were purchased by the Derwent Valley Railway as their Nos 2 and 1, *Lord Wenlock*, respectively, No D2245 has since been sold to the Market Bosworth Light Railway, where it now resides. An earlier member of the class No D2207 is on the North Yorkshire Moors Railway. The details in parenthesis refer to the modified design which includes Nos D2245 and D2271.

BR Class 4MT 2–6–0

Driving wheels: 5ft 3in
Weight: (engine only) 59 tons 2 cwt
Cylinders: 17½in × 26in
Pressure: 225lb
Tractive effort: 24,170lb

One of BR's standard designs, a 2–6–0 for intermediate passenger and miscellaneous duties. A direct development of the LMS 43000 class (see page 112), of which 115 engines were built between 1953 and 1957, Nos 76000 to 76114. No 76017, purchased from Barry Scrapyard and went to Quainton Road, it has since been transfered to the Mid-Hants Railway. No 76079 also from Barry is at Steamport, Southport undergoing restoration.

BR Class 8P 4–6–2 No 71000 'Duke of Gloucester'

Driving wheels: 6ft 2in
Weight: (without tender) 101¼ tons
Cylinders: (3) 18in × 28in
Pressure: 250lb
Tractive effort: 39,080lb

BR's express passenger Pacific designed by Mr R. A. Riddles and built in 1954, but unfortunately destined to be the only one of its kind; before any more could be constructed the decision to abandon steam working had been taken. No 71000 *Duke of Gloucester* was based largely on the LMS 'Duchess' class (see page 105) with four cylinders, but the design was later modified and it eventually appeared as a three-cylinder engine with Caprotti valve gear. Its working life was short. It was withdrawn in November 1962, and after a year or two in storage at Crewe, where its cylinders and motion were removed for preservation, it gravitated to Barry scrapyard without its tender. In 1974 what remained of it, together with a tender from a Class 9F 2–10–0, were obtained by the 71000 (Duke of Gloucester) Steam Locomotive Trust Ltd who are undertaking its restoration on the premises of the GCR Main Line Steam Trust at Loughborough.

BR Class 2MT 2–6–0 1954

Driving wheels: 5ft 0in
Weight: (loco only) 49¼ tons
Cylinders: 16½in × 24in
Pressure: 200lb
Tractive effort: 18,515lb

A British Railways' standard design, almost identical with Ivatt's LMS engines introduced in 1946 (see page 112). It was intended for cross-country lines with severe weight re- strictions, such as the former Cambrian system, but also found on all Regions except the Southern. Sixty-five engines, Nos 78000-78064, were built between 1954 and 1956. No 78019, seen in the illustration at Euston on empty stock working in April 1964, has been acquired by the Severn Valley Railway and No 78022 by the Keighley & Worth Valley Railway. No 78018 has gone to the Market Bosworth Light Railway.

English Electric 'Deltic' Co-Co 1955

Type: Co-Co
Engine: 2 × Napier diesels, 1650hp each
Weight: 106 tons
Driving wheels: 3ft 7in
Tractive effort: 60,000lb

Prototype of the standard class introduced on the Eastern Region in 1961 for the main line between Kings Cross and Edinburgh. Built by English Electric in 1955, works No 2007, and for four years worked trials in the LM Region, although it was never taken into BR stock. The illustration shows it at Euston in 1956. It worked until 1960 when it was presented by English Electric & Napier to the Science Museum, where it can now be seen adjacent to GWR *Caerphilly Castle* of 1923, *Bauxite* of 1874, *The Rocket* and *Sanspareil* of 1829, and *Puffing Billy* of 1814, representing the two extremes of 140 years of the development of rail traction. It is perhaps rather unfortunate that there are no main line representatives of,

say, between 1870 and 1920 to complete the picture.

English Electric diesel-electric shunter No D0226

1956

Engine: English Electric 750rpm 500hp
Weight: 48 tons
Max tractive effort: 33,000lb

One of two experimental engines built by the Vulcan Foundry and English Electric in 1956 (works Nos D226 and 2345 respectively) for comparison purposes, one diesel-electric and the other diesel-hydraulic. The diesel-electric engine No D0226 has now been acquired by the Keighley & Worth Valley Railway, on loan from the English Electric Co Ltd.

BR 0–6–0DM shunter

1956

Driving wheels: 3ft 6in
Weight: 36 tons 7 cwt
Engine: Gardner 204hp
Tractive effort: 16,100lb

Last survivor of a class of 20 engines, built between 1956 and 1961 by Hudswell Clarke. No D2511, built in 1961 (works No D1202) was sold out of service to the NCB and was purchased in 1977 by Ben Wade and A. Stowe, from Broadworth Colliery, Yorkshire. It is now in use on the Keighley & Worth Valley Railway.

BR Caprotti Class 5MT 4–6–0

1956

Driving wheels: 6ft 2in
Weight: 76¼ tons
Cylinders: 19in×28in
Pressure: 225lb
Tractive effort: 26,120lb

Thirty of the BR Standard Class 5MT 4–6–0s (see page 118) Nos 73125-54, were built with Caprotti valve gear. No 73129, turned out from Doncaster in 1956, was secured by Derby Corporation on behalf of the Midland Railway Trust, who have plans for a working line at Butterley, near Ripley.

BR Class 31 diesel-electric A1A-A1A 1957

Engine: English Electric 12SV 1470bhp
Weight: 109 tons
Tractive effort: 42,800lb
Transmission: 4 Brush traction motors

The prototype of this class was the first main line diesel locomotive to be built by Brush Traction for British Railways under their 1955 Modernisation Plan. The 20 locomotives (Nos D5500-19) were later designated as Class 31/0 and subsequent batches with detail differences are still in service. No D5500 (renum- bered 31.018) was withdrawn from service in 1976 and restored to original green livery for display at the National Railway Museum, York. However, it spent only a short time there before being placed on loan to the North Yorkshire Moors Railway. It ran to Grosmont under its own power, hauling the preserved 'Q7' 0–8–0 which is being restored on the NYMR, and has since been employed on pas- senger services between Grosmont and Pickering.

SR Rebuilt 'West Country' 4–6–2　　　1957

Driving wheels: 6ft 2in
Weight: 90 tons
Cylinders: (3) 16³/₈in×24in
Pressure: 250lb
Tractive effort: 27,715lb

Of the lighter version of Bulleid's somewhat revolutionary Pacifics, 60 of the 110 were rebuilt on more conventional lines, as were all of the larger 'Merchant Navies'. Several in unrebuilt form have been preserved. Of the modified ones, No 34101 is illustrated. It was built at Brighton in 1950, receiving the name *Hartland*. It was rebuilt in September 1960. Rescued from Barry scrapyard in 1978, it is destined for the proposed Peak Park Railway. No 34016 *Bodmin* is on the Mid-Hants Railway, No 34049 *Boscastle* is with the GCR Main Line Steam Trust, No 34053 *Sir Keith Park* is to go to the Bournemouth Steam Centre, No 34059 *Sir Archibald Sinclair* is on the Bluebell Railway.

BR Class 03 0–6–0 diesel shunter　　　1957

Engine: Gardner 8L3 204bhp
Weight: 30 tons
Tractive effort: 15,300lb
Transmission: Vulcan-Sinclair fluid coupling and Wilson-Drewry 5 speed gearbox

As the standard 204hp diesel shunter for British Railways, more than 200 of these locomotives were built and less than half now remain in service. They were built by BR workshops and had a Gardner engine and mechanical transmission. Four examples have so far been preserved, No D2117 on the Lakeside Railway where it was renumbered 8, No D2192 on the Dart Valley Railway, and No D2381 at Steamtown, Carnforth. The fourth, No 03.090 (originally D2090) is used for mar-

shalling exhibits at the National Railway Museum, York.

BR Class 24 diesel-electric Bo-Bo 1958

Engine: Sulzer 6LDA28 1,160bhp
Weight: 77-9 tons
Tractive effort: 40,000lb
Transmission: Four BTH 137 BY traction motors

The BR Derby/Sulzer Type 2 was adopted as the standard Type 2 diesel electric locomotive and 150 examples were built, followed by further similar locomotives with uprated engines and detail differences. They were numbered D5000-5150 and became Nos 24.001-150 under the 1968 renumbering, (four members of the class having been scrapped). The last few survivors in BR service lasted into 1979. The one example so far preserved was loaned to the North Yorkshire Moors Railway during the drought of 1976 when fire risk prevented steam locomotive operation. It is owned by a scrap metal merchant who has now extended its term of loan to the NYMR. The locomotive has been repainted in two-tone green and returned to its original number, D5032.

BR Class 42 'Warship' B-B 1958

Wheel diameter: 3ft 3½in
Weight: 78 tons
Tractive effort: 52,400lb

One of the earliest main line diesel classes introduced by British Railways in 1958 as part of a large conversion plan to eliminate steam working, a project which was in fact completed by 1968. These locomotives, like some others which were built specifically for use on the Western Region, had hydraulic instead of the more usual electric transmission. The 'Warship' class became extinct in 1972. There were 76 engines in all, Nos D800 to D870, together with five predecessors, Nos D600 to D604. Some were built at Swindon and others by the North British Locomotive Company.

No D821 *Greyhound* was obtained in 1973

by the Diesel Traction Group, and is at present located at Swindon as illustrated. No D832 *Onslaught* has been purchased from Derby Testing Centre and is possibly destined for the North Yorkshire Moors Railway. One of the earlier 'Warships' No 601 *Ark Royal*, remains in Barry Scrapyard.

BR Class 71 electric Bo-Bo — 1958

Equipment: Four English Electric 638hp traction motors
Weight: 77 tons
Tractive effort: 43,000lb

This class originally consisted of 24 locomotives (Nos E5000-23), built at Doncaster for use on the newly electrified South Eastern Section lines of the Southern Region. They were used on freight services and on the 'Night Ferry' and 'Golden Arrow' trains. Ten of the class were later rebuilt as electro-diesel locomotives for duties on the Waterloo-Bournemouth line. The Class 71s were fitted with pick-up shoes for 750V dc operation, and also with a pantograph for use in sidings equipped with overhead catenary. All were withdrawn by the end of 1977 and No 71.001 (formerly E5001) was despatched to Doncaster for repainting prior to its acquisition by the National Railway Museum, York. The illustration shows No E5000, the first of the class

BR Class 02 0–4–0 shunter — 1960

Engine: Rolls-Royce C6NFL 179bhp
Weight: 28 tons
Tractive effort: 15,000lb
Transmission: Rolls-Royce torque converter and Yorkshire Engine Co final drive

A class of 20 small shunting locomotives with hydraulic transmission built by the Yorkshire Engine Company and numbered D2850-69. All have been withdrawn from service but No D2860 is at the National Railway Museum, York, not yet on public display. The illustration shows No D2852.

BR Class 9F 2–10–0   1954

Driving wheels: 5ft 0in
Weight: 86 tons 14 cwt
Cylinders: (2) 20in × 28in
Pressure: 250lb
Tractive effort: 39,670lb

British Railways' final design before the decision to abandon steam was made, and in many ways one of the most efficient and successful of all. In all 251 of them were constructed between 1954 and 1960, the last one No 92220 was built at Swindon in March of that year, being very appropriately named *Evening Star*, and was finished in BR lined green livery with a copper capped chimney. Withdrawn in 1965 after a working life of only five years, it was set aside for preservaton. Following several periods of loan to the Keighley & Worth Valley Railway and use on BR main line railtours it is now at the National Railway Museum, York. No 92203, now named *Black Prince*, is on the East Somerset Railway at Cranmore and No 92240 on the Bluebell Railway. No 92212 is on the GCR Main Line Steam Trust. No 92214 has also been purchased for preservation.

BR Class 84 electric Bo-Bo   1960

Equipment: Four GEC motors, 3,100hp continuous rating
Weight: 75.5 tons
Maximum tractive effort: 50,000lb

After spending most of its life on the West Coast route No 84.001 was withdrawn from service at Crewe electric depot early in 1979, and was obtained by the National Railway Museum for display at York. The illustration shows the locomotive in its original condition and numbered E3036.

BR Class 35 'Hymek' diesel-hydrauic B-B   1961

Engine: Bristol-Siddeley/Maybach MD870. 1700bhp
Weight: 75 tons
Tractive effort: 49,700lb
Transmission: Stone-Maybach Mekydro

The Beyer Peacock 'Hymek' class consisted of 101 locomotives, introduced in 1961 and numbered from D7000-D7100. Though designated as Type 3, medium power locomotives, they were lively performers, employed first

on many Paddington-South Wales services, and later on Worcester line duties. The entire class was withdrawn during the elimination of the BR diesel-hydraulic fleet, but three examples survive. No D7029 was acquired by the Diesel Traction Group and is kept at BREL, Swindon, while Nos D7017/8 are preserved by the Diesel and Electric Group, the former on the West Somerset Railway and the latter at Didcot Railway Centre.

BR Class 52 'Western' diesel-hydraulic C-C   1961

Engines: Two Maybach MD655. 1350bhp each
Weight: 109 tons
Tractive effort: 72,600lb
Transmission: Two Voith-North British hydraulic transmissions

A class of 74 locomotives (Nos D1000-73), built at Swindon and Crewe for Western

Region main line service. The first examples were painted in experimental colour schemes before maroon was adopted as standard for the class. All carried names incorporating the word 'Western', and as the last main diesel-hydraulic locomotives all were withdrawn between 1973-7. Owing to their great popularity among enthusiasts a number of the last active 'Westerns' were acquired for preservation. No D1023 *Western Fusilier* is now in the National Railway Museum, York, while sisters Nos D1013 *Western Ranger* and D1062 *Western Courier* are preserved by the Western Locomotive Association on the Severn Valley Railway. No D1010 *Western Campaigner* is privately preserved at the premises of Foster Yeoman at Merehead Quarry and may be renamed *Western Yeoman*. Two others, acquired more recently are Nos D1048 *Western Lady* and D1041 *Western Prince* which are now on the North York Moors Railway. Among those awaiting scrapping at BREL, Swindon, No D1015 *Western Champion* may be acquired for preservation.

BR Class 07 0–6–0 diesel-electric   1962

Engine: Paxman 6-cyl RPHL
Weight: 42 ton
Maximum tractive effort: 28,240lb

Designed for shunting in the Southampton Docks complex, and built by Ruston & Hornsby in 1962, it replaced the USA 0–6–0T engines previously employed. The last of the class were withdrawn in 1977 with several being sold out of service for industrial use. At the time of writing the only member of the class preserved is No 07.010 (D2294) on the West Somerset Railway.

Part Three

Hawthorne 0–4–0WT 'Ellesmere' 1861

Driving wheels: 3ft 6½in
Cylinders: 12in × 18in

Built by Hawthorne's of Leith in 1861 (works No 244) this is the oldest surviving locomotive to have been built in Scotland. Withdrawn from service in 1957 from Howe Bridge Colliery, Leigh, Lancashire, and purchased jointly by the Stephenson Loco Society, Manchester Loco Society and J. H. Farr. Now at the premises of the Scottish Railway Preservation Society, and on view in its Museum in Falkirk.

Stephen Lewin 0–4–0ST Seaham Harbour No 18 1863

Built by Stephen Lewin, Dorset Foundry, Poole, Dorset in 1863. By the 1950s it was employed at Seaham Harbour, Durham; it was sent to Beamish Museum in 1975. The engine has been completely rebuilt at Beamish and the illustration shows the engine in its present condition.

Coalbrookdale No 5

1865

Driving wheels: 3ft 0in
Cylinders: 12in × 15in
Pressure: 100lb

Built at the Company's own works in 1865, where it worked until 1932. It was reboilered by the Lilleshall Co in 1925, and sold to Bardon Hill Quarries (Ellis & Everard Ltd); it was in service there until 1956. It was returned to Coalbrookdale in 1959 and preserved at its makers' works. It was later moved to the Ironbridge Gorge Museum where it is now on display.

Neilson 0–4–0WT Gas Light & Coke Company No 1

1870

Driving wheels: 2ft 9in
Cylinders: 10in × 18in

Built by Nelson & Co in 1870 (works No 1561) for the extensive system first opened by the Gas Light and Coke Company at Beckton, East London at that period. No 1 formerly named *Alderman* was acquired in 1963 by the Industrial Locomotive Society and is now in the Industrial Railway Museum at Penrhyn Castle, Bangor.

Head Wrightson vertical boiler 0–4–0

Driving wheels: 2ft 4in
Cylinders: 6in × 12in
Geared Ratio: 3:1

Several of these small machines – usually nicknamed 'coffeepots' – were built by Head Wrightson in the 1870s, and three of them have after many years of service been preserved. The two illustrated were Nos 16 and 17 of the Seaham Harbour Dock Co, where they worked until their withdrawal about 1960. They were makers No 21 of 1870 and No 33 of 1873, and it will be seen that they differ in that the earlier engine has vertical cylinders with the drive through intermediate gearing; the other has inclined cylinders with direct drive. Another of the geared type (to which the dimensional particulars quoted apply) was built in 1871. The works plate reads 'T. H. Head Engineer 90 Cannon St London 1871'. It is now housed in the Beamish Museum, Durham. This locomotive was owned by the Dorking Greystone Lime Company, Betchworth, Surrey, and although it had not worked for some time when the quarry ceased to use

rail traction in 1960, it was still in existence and has now been returned to the builders and restored. The first illustration shows No 16, and the other, No 17. No 16 is preserved by the makers at Thornaby, No 17 is at Darlington North Road Museum and No 21 at Eaglescliffe Museum.

Aveling & Porter engines

Aveling & Porter constructed a large number of these two-cylinder compound geared locomotives for light shunting and six interesting examples have survived, four of the more usual 0–4–0 variety. The earliest of these is

the Oxford & Aylesbury Tramroad engine now to be found in the London Transport Museum, Covent Garden. Two of the last engines of this type to remain at work were owned by the British Oil & Cake Mills, Erith. *Sydenham*

works No 3567 of 1895, is now on loan to the Quainton Road Society. The very similar *Sir Vincent*, works No 8800 of 1917, is now working on the Hollycombe Woodland Railway.

The other two locomotives are single wheelers. Works No 9449 of 1926 is a single-cylinder geared engine. It was built in 1926 (works No 9449) for the Portland Cement Works, Snodland, Kent. Now named *Blue Circle* it is preserved at Sheffield Park, on the Bluebell Railway. Another 220T *Excelsior*, 1607 of 1880. of 3ft gauge, is at Donington Park, Castle Donington, Derby.

Peckett 0–6–0WT 'Secundus'

1872

Driving wheels: 2ft 3in
Cylinders: 7in diameter
Gauge: 2ft 8in

The second engine owned by this company working the china clay deposits in Dorset,

Secundus was built in 1872 by Bellis and Seekings, and rebuilt by Peckett & Sons in 1933. It was retired in 1955 and now rests in the Birmingham Museum of Science and Industry. The illustration shows it in May 1955 when it was still in use in Dorset.

Black Hawthorn 0–4–0ST 'Bauxite'

1874

Driving wheels: 2ft 9in
Weight: 12 tons
Cylinders: 9in × 16in

Built by Black Hawthorn & Co in 1874 (works No 305). Owned by the Industrial Aluminium Co Ltd at their Hebburn Chemical works. It

was withdrawn in 1947, and presented by ICI to the North East Historical & Industrial Locomotive Society. In 1953 it went to the Science Museum in South Kensington, being chosen as representative of the industrial locomotive era of the 19th century.

Fox Walker 0–6–0ST   1874

This 0–6–0ST was built in 1874 by Fox Walker & Co (works No 242). It was rebuilt in 1891, and again in 1903, it worked at the Mountain Ash Colliery as No 3 until the early 1960s. It was preserved for some time on the premises of the Somerset & Dorset Railway Circle, Radstock, then moved to Bitton, Bristol Suburban Railway, it is scheduled for removal to the Bristol Industrial Museum, at Princess Wharf, Bristol.

R. Evans & Co 0–6–0WT Haydock Collieries 'Bellerophon'   1874

Driving wheels: 4ft 0in
Weight: 35 tons
Cylinders: 16in×22in
Pressure: 140lb
Tractive effort: 13,950lb

One of six 0–6–0WTs built by Richard Evans &

Co at Haydock foundry for the Haydock Collieries, *Bellerophon* having been produced in 1874, works letter C, presumably the third locomotive built by the firm. It worked until 1964, latterly at Lea Green Colliery, and has now been acquired by the Keighley & Worth Valley Railway at Haworth.

Manning Wardle 0–6–0ST No 4   1877

Driving wheels: 3ft 0in
Weight: 23 tons
Cylinders: 20in×10in
Pressure: 125lb

A good example of the earlier Manning Wardle standard type of engine for industrial work, built in 1877 (works No 641). It was eventually

acquired by Samuel Williams & Sons Ltd of Dagenham, Essex as No 4. Now preserved at Bressingham Hall, Diss. Another very similar engine, built in 1883 (works No 865) *Aldwyth*, formerly owned by the Ministry of Public Building and Works, is now on the Gwili Railway, Carmarthen.

de Winton & Chaplin vertical boiler 0–4–0WT   1877

Driving wheels: 1ft 8in
Cylinders: 6¼in × 12in
Chaloner only

Two firms which specialised in vertical boiler engines, mainly for the narrow gauge system of the quarries in North Wales. Several have been preserved. *George Henry* and *Kathleen* both built in 1877 for Penrhyn Quarries are, respectively, at the Narrow Gauge Museum at Towyn, and at Blaenau Ffestiniog. *Chaloner* (Pen-y-Orsedd Quarries) now works on the Leighton Buzzard Narrow Gauge Rail-

way. Currently on loan to the National Railway Museum.

Pendyffryn (1894, Pen-y-Orsedd), owned by A. J. Hills, is at Pontsticill together with a 2ft gauge Chaplin engine built at Redstone, Penmaenmawr in 1905. *Watkin* (1893, Penmaenmawr Quarries) is in the Industrial Railway Museum at Penrhyn Castle. A standard gauge engine of this type built by Chaplin (2368 of 1885) for Northampton Gasworks is now at Nottingham Industrial Museum, Wollaton Hall.

Fletcher Jennings & Co 0–4–0T
Dorking Greystone Lime Company   1877

Driving wheels: 3ft 6in
Cylinders: 12in × 20in

Built by Fletcher Jennings & Co in 1877 (works No 158) for use on the lower part of the quarry system at Betchworth, Surrey. It continued

work until rail operation was abandoned in 1960, when it was acquired on loan by the Bluebell Railway and may be seen at their headquarters at Sheffield Park. The illustration shows the engine, No 3 *Baxter* at Sheffield Park, prior to restoration.

Beyer Peacock works engine   1879

Driving wheels: 3ft 0½in
Weight: (as 0–4–0ST) 21 tons
Cylinders: 12in × 18in
Pressure: 130lb

This engine is one of several built by Messrs Beyer Peacock & Co for industrial use. This

one, works No 1827, stock No 3701, of 1879, was retained by the company for its own use as a works shunter, which it performed for the whole of its life until 1966. Between the 1880s and until after World War II it was fitted with a crane and ran as a 0–4–2ST. The other five similar engines built between 1879 and 1910 were used by various British industrial firms but one was of 5ft 6in gauge used in Buenos Aires. Formerly preserved by Mr R. Bedson at Ward End Works, Poynton, Cheshire, it is now at the Cambrian Railways Society's premises at Oswestry.

Stephenson & Co 0–6–0T 'Haydock'   1879

Built by Stephenson & Co in 1879 (works No 2309), and latterly worked at the Haydock Collieries, Lancashire, when it acquired the name *Haydock*. It is now in the Industrial Railway Museum at Penrhyn Castle, Bangor.

Hunslet 0–4–0ST Penrhyn Railway   1882

Driving wheels: 2ft 1in
Weight: 12¼ tons
Cylinders: 10½in×12in
Pressure: 140lb
Tractive effort: 6,320lb
Gauge: 1ft 11½in

Three engines owned by the Penrhyn Quarries, Bethesda, Caernarvon, for working its five-mile main line down to Port Penrhyn. They were built by the Hunslet Engine Co, *Charles* in 1882 (works No 283), and *Blanche* and *Linda* in 1893 (works Nos 589 and 590). This section

of the system was abandoned in 1962, since when *Charles* has been placed in the Industrial Railway Museum, Penrhyn Castle, and his two sisters have been purchased by the Festiniog Railway rebuilt as 2–4–0Ts with tenders, and vacuum brakes for working passenger trains.

Avonside Engine Co Guinness 0–4–0T narrow gauge   1882

Driving wheels: 1ft 10in
Weight: 7 tons 8 cwt
Cylinders: 7in × 8½in
Pressure: 180lb
Tractive effort: 2,900lb
Gauge: 1ft 10in

The well-known brewing firm of Arthur Guinness Son & Co Ltd had 19 narrow gauge locomotives for working around its extensive premises in Dublin. The first engine, No 6 was constructed by the Avonside Engine Co in 1882, but Nos 7 to 24, which followed between 1887 and 1920, were all built in Ireland by W. Spence, of Cork Street Foundry, Dublin. Several have been preserved, No 13 in the Narrow Gauge Railway Museum at Towyn, No 15 by the Irish Steam Preservation Society at Stradbally, Leitrim, No 23 at the Narrow

Gauge Railway Museum, Blaenau Ffestiniog. No 20 in Belfast Museum, whilst No 17 is preserved by Guinness themselves at their Dublin premises.

Neilson 0–4–0ST   1882

Driving wheels: 3ft 8in
Cylinders: 14in × 20in
Pressure: 120lb

Built by Neilson & Co in 1876 (works No 2203) No 13 of the Gartshore Colliery, Glasgow, has

been presented by the NCB to the Scottish Railway Preservation Society (illustrated). Built in 1882 (works No 2937) for the Gartsherries Ironworks, Glasgow, their No 11 is now at Chasewater.

Hunslet 0–4–0STs Penrhyn and Dinorwic Railways

1883

Driving wheels: 1ft 8in
Weight: 6¾ tons
Cylinders: 7in × 20in
Tractive effort: 2,940lb
Gauge: 1ft 10¾in (Dinorwic) 1ft 11½in (Penrhyn)

The Hunslet Engine Company built 35 engines of very similar basic design, with some variations in detail, between 1883 and 1932 for the extensive slate quarry systems at Bethesda and Llanberis in North Wales. On the abandonment of rail traction in the quarries during the 1950s and 1960s the engines were much sought after by various bodies, and the great majority of them have been preserved, some

even having gone to America. Full particulars of these will be found in the tabulated section devoted to the Hunslet Engine Company. The general dimensions are applicable to the class as a whole, but vary slightly with individual engines, The illustration shows *Gwynedd*, now to be found at Bressingham Hall, when it was at work in Penrhyn Quarries in 1953. Four of the Dinorwic engines now work on the Llanberis Lake Railway, 1ft 10½ gauge line using the trackbed of the Padarn Railway. They have been fitted with cabs, as shown in the illustration of *Dolbadarn*. In their quarry days most of the engines ran cabless. The Llanberis Lake Railway engines are: *Red Damsel* (renamed *Elidir*), *Wild Aster*, and *Dolbadarn*. *Dorothea*

and *Una* are going to the Brecon Mountain Railway, Pontsicill, *Holy War, Alice* and *Maid Marion* are on the Bala Lake Railway. The liveries of the Dinorwic and Penrhyn Railways were red and green respectively, but under their new ownerships whilst some may adhere to the original, others will vary considerably according to the owners' personal tastes.

Black, Hawthorn 0–4–0ST 'Kettering Furnaces No 3'

1885

Gauge: 3ft 0in

Built by Black, Hawthorn in 1885 (works No 859) for the narrow gauge system connecting the ironstone quarry with the furnaces at Kettering (now entirely demolished), two miles north of the MR main line on the west side. The quarries finally closed in 1963, and No 3 is now preserved in the Industrial Railway Museum at Penrhyn Castle, Bangor.

Beyer Peacock 0–4–0 tram

1886

A standard steam tram locomotive of the period, built by Beyer Peacock & Co in 1886 (works No 2734) for the Manchester, Bury, Rochdale & Oldham Steam Tramway No 84, and subsequently acquired by the Ince Wagon & Ironworks, Ince, Lancashire. Presented to British Railways in 1955 for preservation, now part of the National Railway Museum's collection but at present on loan to the Dinting Railway Centre.

Manning Wardle 0–6–0ST 'Kettering Furnaces No 8'

1889

Gauge: 3ft 0in

One of three 0–6–0STs with outside cylinders built by Manning Wardle & Co for the Kettering Iron and Coal Co. The earliest of them No 6 was built in 1889, followed by No 7 in 1897, and No 8 in 1906 (works No 1675). The system finally closed in 1963, and No 8 is preserved by the Welland Valley Traction Club at Market Harborough.

Manning Wardle 0–6–0ST 'Sir Berkeley' 1890

Driving wheels: 3ft 0in
Weight: 19 tons
Cylinders: 12in × 18in
Pressure: 140lb
Tractive effort: 8,680lb

Built by Manning Wardle & Co in 1890 (works No 1210) for Logan and Hemmingway, Contractors. One of that firm's standard designs of locomotive for general industrial work. This particular engine, which became Logan and Hemmingway's No 30 (later No 10), was employed for many years at various sites on railway construction work, notably the MS&LR in Nottinghamshire, later the Great Central extension to London and the GWR Westbury and Frome avoiding lines in 1931-33. It had been rebuilt by the makers in 1910, and in 1935 was sold to the Cranford Ironstone Co in Northants, where it was at work until the early 1960s. Purchased in 1963 by Mr R. Crombleholme and now kept at Haworth, K&WVR.

Stephenson & Co 0–6–0ST 1891

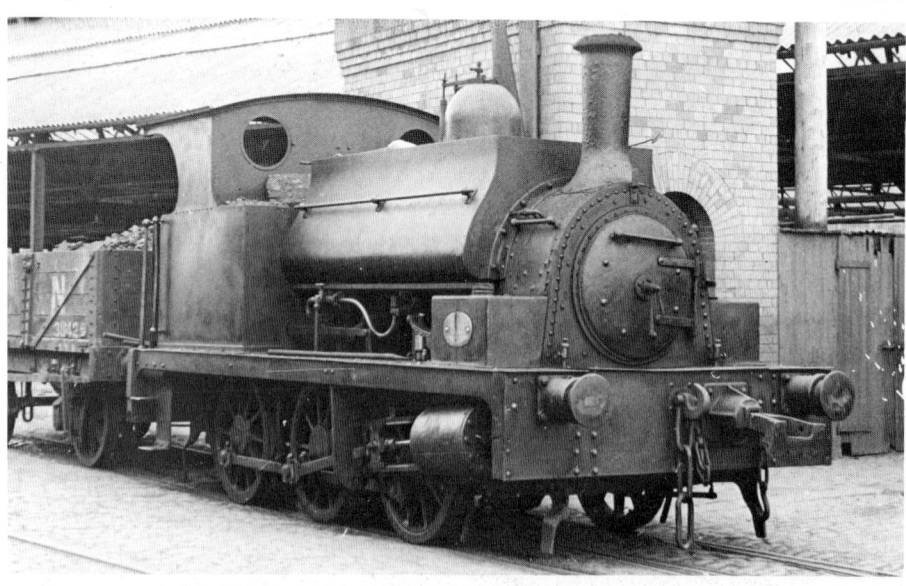

Built by Stephenson & Co in 1891 (works No 2738) for shunting the Londonderry Port & Harbour Commissioners quayside at Londonderry. Now in Belfast Museum.

Neilson 0–4–0T
1892

Built by Neilson & Co in 1892 (works No 4444) for the By-Products section of Beckton Gasworks, East London. The engines were left quite apart from those in the main works, and were numbered in a separate series. It so happens that both No 1's have been preserved, (see page 130 for the 1870 engine). This later one has been purchased privately and is now at Bressingham Hall, Diss, Norfolk.

Bagnall 0–4–0ST
1897

Driving wheels: 16½in
Weight: 5¼ tons
Cylinders: 6in dia
Most of these engines are of 2ft 0in gauge.

Several engines of a standard type of saddle tank built by Bagnall & Sons Ltd for narrow gauge industrial systems have survived.
No 1491 of 1897 *Isabel* on plinth outside Stafford Station.
No 2067 of 1917 *Peter* is preserved by NGC Blaenau Ffestiniog.
No 2087 of 1919 *Leonard* in the Birmingham Science Museum.

No 2088 of 1919 *Lady Luxborough* at Henley-in-Arden.
No 2090 of 1919 *Pixie* on Cadeby Light Railway.
No 2091 of 1919 *Wendy* acquired by Hampshire Light Railway Museum, Durley.
No 2133 of 1924 *Woto* and No 2135 of 1925 *Sir Tom* both from Callender's Cables, Belvedere, preserved by P. Elms, Romford.
(The illustration shows *Pixie* at Cadeby in 1975.)

Hunslet 0–6–0T   1898

Driving wheels: 3ft 5in
Weight: 35 tons
Cylinder: 15½in × 20in
Pressure: 160lb
Tractive effort: 15,940lb

Built by the Hunslet Engine Co in 1898 (works No 686) for the Manchester Ship Canal as

their No 14 *St Johns*. Later sold to ICI Dyestuffs Division, Blackley, Manchester. Purchased 1969 by the Warwickshire Industrial Locomotive Preservation Group, named *The Lady Armaghdale,* and painted in Midland livery of crimson lake lined out black and yellow. Kept at Bridgnorth, Severn Valley Railway.

Borrows 0–4–0WTs   1898

Driving wheels: 3ft 4in
Weight: 25 tons
Cylinders: 14½in × 20in
Pressure: 60lb
Tractive effort: 14,300lb
(These dimensions apply to *Windle*, the others may vary somewhat.)

Borrows & Sons of St Helen's, Lancs succeeded Cross & Co who specialised in a small type of well tank for industrial work, chiefly in Lancashire and Cheshire. Three examples have survived for preservation, *The King,* built in 1906 for Nuttall & Co, St Helens, (works No 48) went in 1923 to United Glass Bottle Manu-

facturers Limited of Charlton, Kent. It is now at Market Bosworth, headquarters of the Shackerstone Railway Society. The earliest engine, built in 1898 (works No 37), which was Wallsend Slipway No 3, is now on the North Yorkshire Moors Railway. *Windle*, shown in the illustration, was built in 1909 for use at the works of Pilkington Brothers of St Helens, where it remained in service until 1961, in which year it was presented to the Middleton Railway Trust and is now at their premises near Leeds. A similar engine built by Kerr Stuart & Company in 1918 (works No 3063) is to be found at Fairfield's, Chepstow.

Barclay 0—4—0T   1899

Driving wheels: 1ft 10in
Weight: 7½ tons
Cylinders: 6½in × 12in

Pressure: 120lb
Gauge: 3ft 0in

One of two engines built by Andrew Barclay of Kilmarnock in 1899 (works Nos 839 and 840) for contractors' use. No 840 worked on various sites for many years, reservoir construction and so on, in Shropshire, Wales and Scotland; and was finally presented by the British Aluminium Co to the Scottish Railway Preservation Society, for exhibition at its museum in Falkirk.

Neilson 0–4–0ST

Driving wheels: 3ft 6in
Weight: 23½ tons
Cylinders: 14in×21in
Pressure: 150lb

One of several saddle tanks built by Neilson for shunting in the Bass & Co's well-known brewery yards and through the streets at Burton-on-Trent. No 9 was built in 1901 (works No 5907). Now preserved at the Bass Museum at Burton-on-Trent. Livery, brick red.

Kerr Stuart 0–4–0WT

Driving wheels: 1ft 8in
Weight: 3 tons
Pressure: 140lb
Gauge: 2ft 0in

Formerly owned by the Dundee Gasworks, this locomotive was, on withdrawal in 1959, purchased by Ian Fraser of Arbroath. It was built by Kerr Stuart in 1900 (works No 720) and now carries the nameplate *Bonnie Dundee*. A similar engine (works No 721 of 1902) was presented by the Scottish Gas Board in 1959 to the Narrow Gauge Railway Museum at Towyn. Details of other very similar engines from Provan gasworks, Glasgow, and Granton, Edinburgh, will be found in the Andrew Barclay works list, Nos 984, 988, 1871 and 1890.

Barclay crane tank 0–4–0CT   1902

Combined engine and crane of a type once used to some extent not only by industrial concerns, particularly steelworks and the like, but also by some main line railways as works engines, such as the Great Eastern, Great Western and others, but none of which have survived. This locomotive was built by Andrew Barclay in 1902 (works No 880) and was owned by Messrs Glenfield & Kennedy Limited, of Kilmarnock. Restored by McAlpines in 1968 and is now at the Steamtown, Carnforth.

Peckett 0–6–0ST

1903

Gauge: 1ft 11½in

One of a series of 0–6–0STs built by Peckett & Sons for the Rugby Portland Cement Co, Southam, Warwick. *Jurassic* (works No 1008 of 1903), works on the Lincolnshire Coast Light Railway near Grimsby, whilst a second

Mesozoic (works No 1327 of 1913) is owned by A. J. Hills, Llanberis, and is to go to the Brecon Mountain Railway Pontsticill. A third, *Liassic* (works No 1632 of 1923) was sent to Canada in 1959. While *Triassic* (No 1272 of 1911) now works on the Knebworth Park Railway.

Hudswell Clarke 0–6–0T

1903

Driving wheels: 3ft 3in
Weight: 32 tons 14 cwt
Cylinders: 15½in×20in
Pressure: 140lb
Tractive effort: 14,660lb

Built by Hudswell Clarke & Co in 1903 (works No 679) for the Manchester Ship Canal, on which system it was No 31, known as *Hamburg*, the name being carried, as on this railway's locomotives, most unusually inside the

cab. The name is now carried on name plates on the tank sides. Now acquired by the Keighley & Worth Valley Railway, which also has another locomotive, No 67 built by Hudswell Clarke in 1919 (works No 1369). Two other engines Nos 32 *Gothenburg*, and 70 (works Nos 680 and 1464) are preserved by the East Lancashire Preservation Society, Bury.

Kerr Stuart 0–4–2ST 1905

Driving wheels: 3ft 9in
Cylinders: 9in×15in
Pressure: 160lb
Tractive effort: 5,508lb
Gauge: 2ft 6in

Four engines built by Kerr Stuart & Co between 1905 and 1924 for the large paper works at Sittingbourne, Kent, later known as Bowaters Lloyd Pulp & Paper Mills. The company ceased rail operation in 1969, but part of the line has been taken over by the Locomotive Club of Great Britain and is now worked as a pleasure line, The Sittingbourne & Kemsley Light Railway. *Premier* and *Leader*, Kerr Stuart works Nos 886 and 926 of 1905, the two original engines, together with *Melior*, works No 4219 of 1924, are still at Sittingbourne. The last mentioned, which is illustrated, is interesting in being fitted with Hackworth valve gear. The fourth engine, *Excelsior*, works No 1049 of 1908, is now on the Whipsnade Zoo Railway.

Peckett 0–4–0T 1906

Driving wheels: 1ft 8in
Weight: 7 tons
Cylinders: 7in×10in
Pressure: 160lb
Gauge: 3ft 0in

One of three locomotives built by Peckett & Sons for the British Aluminium Co, Larne Harbour, No 2 in 1906 (works No 1097) is now in Belfast Museum. The illustration shows a sister engine, No 1 (Peckett 1904 works No 1026), on a pleasure railway at Shanes Castle, Antrim, where it is now known as No 1 *Tyrone*.

The second locomotive is one of the three Bord Na Mona tank engines depicted on page 161, No 3 now named *Shane*. These engines were in service until about 1956.

Avonside 0–6–0T 'Nancy'

1908

Gauge: 3ft 0in

0–6–0T *Nancy*, built by the Avonside Engine Co in 1908 (works No 1547) for the Eastwell Iron Ore Co, Leicester. The rail system closed in 1906, and the engine was preserved by Stirland Brothers, Watnall, Notts. It has now gone to Shanes Castle Railway, Antrim.

Barclay 0–4–0ST 1911

Built by Andrew Barclay & Son in 1911 (works No 1223) for Tharsis Sulphur & Copper Co Ltd, Hebburn, Durham. Resold 1939 to N. Greening & Sons Ltd, Britannia Wire Cloth Works, Warrington. Known as *Colin McAndrews*, it was acquired in 1968 by the Railway Preservation Society, Chasewater, Staffs.

Manning Wardle 0–4–0ST 1912

Driving wheels: 2ft 10in
Cylinders: 16in × 22in
Pressure: 140lb

The only Manning Wardle standard gauge four-coupled engine to have survived is *Brill*, No 14, built in 1912 (works No 1795). It went

new to Messrs T. W. Ward of Sheffield, then moved in 1913 to Lysaght's Park Steel Works, Scunthorpe, later to Wensley Quarries, Preston-under-Scar, North Yorks, and finally to the South Durham Iron and Steel Co's works at Irchester, Northants. It was purchased in 1969 by a group of Quainton Railway Society members and was to be seen at Quainton Road until 1977 when it was transferred to the Northants Ironstone Trust at Hunsbury Hill.

Kerr Stuart 'Wren' Class 0–4–0ST   1918

Driving wheels: 20in
Cylinders: 6in×9in
Pressure: 140lb
Gauge: 2ft 0in

A standard design of narrow gauge locomotive by Kerr Stuart for light industrial work. No 314 of 1918 is preserved at the Narrow Gauge Museum, Blaenau Ffestiniog. Three others, Nos 4250, 4256 and 4260 of 1922 from the Devon County Council, are respectively

Lorna Doone preserved in Birmingham Science Museum, *Peter Pan* and *Pixie*, were on the Leighton Buzzard Light Railway; the latter is illustrated, but before receiving its name. *Peter Pan* was transferred to the Islands Narrow Gauge Museum, Isle of Wight, until 1977. Since then it has been hired out, having been brought back to the mainland, to various private railways around the country.

Barclay 0–6–0T 'The Doll'   1919

Driving wheel: 24in
Cylinder: 7in×14in
Pressure: 160lb
Weight: 8½ tons
Tractive effort: 4,573lb
Gauge: 2ft

The Doll was built by Andrew Barclay in 1918 (works No 1641) for Sydenham Ironstone, Kings Sutton, Oxford, later transferred to Stewart & Lloyds, Bilston. After a short time at Bressingham Hall it was purchased in 1969 by Mr H. Williams for use on the LBLR.

Kerr Stuart 0–6–2T

1920

Driving wheels: 2ft 3in
Cylinders: 10in × 15in
Pressure: 160lb
Tractive effort: 7,555lb
Gauge: 2ft 6in

Note: *Conqueror* is a somewhat larger engine with increased dimensions.

Five 0–6–2Ts were built for Bowaters Paper Mills Factory at Sittingbourne, Kent. The first of these, *Superior*, was constructed by Kerr Stuart in 1920 (works No 4034), followed by four very similar engines from Bagnalls, *Conqueror* in 1922 (works No 2192), *Alpha* in 1932 (2472), *Triumph* (illustrated) in 1934 (2511) and *Superb* in 1940 (2624). The line was closed by Bowaters for commercial use in 1969, but part of it continues to be operated by the Locomotive Club of Great Britain as a pleasure line, retaining some of the engines. This includes the last three of these 0–6–2Ts. The others, the original *Superior*, together with *Conqueror*, are now on the Whipsnade Zoo Railway, their Nos 3 and 4.

Peckett 1287 class 0–4–0T

1923

Driving wheels: 2ft 3in
Weight: 12 tons
Cylinders: 8in × 12in
Pressure: 160lb
Tractive effort: 3,860lb

Built by Peckett & Sons in 1923 (works No 1631). An unusual design for this firm, which usually specialised in robust saddle tanks for heavy industrial work. It was owned by Hardman & Holden of Manchester, and was known as *Marcia*. Presented to the Kent and East Sussex Railway in 1963.

Barclay crane tank 0–4–0CT

1925

Built by Andrew Barclay in 1925, works No 1875, for the Stanton Ironworks. It is now with the Midland Railway Trust at Butterley. The illustration shows it in August 1977 together with the only surviving engine from the firm of Markham & Co, Chesterfield, (works No 109 of 1894). Now named *Gladys* it was built for the Staveley Coal and Iron Co. It is also preserved at Butterley.

Manning Wardle 0–6–0ST 1926

Driving wheels: 3ft 6in
Cylinders: 14in×20in
Weight: 30 tons
Pressure: 160lb
Tractive effort: 12,695lb

The last engine built by the old established firm of Manning Wardle & Co Ltd in 1926 (works No 2047). It was for the Rugby Portland Cement Co, Warwicks. Purchased 1968 by the Warwickshire Industrial Locomotive Preservation Group and kept at Bridgnorth. Now named *Warwickshire* and painted in royal blue livery. Other late Manning Wardle engines are *Abernant* (works No 2015 of 1921) formerly owned by the Austin Motor Works, is now preserved in Birmingham in a playground at Newdigate Street, and No 2025 of 1923 *Winston Churchill* at the Black Country Museum, Dudley.

Kerr Stuart diesels 1929

One of the first diesel locomotives in this country. It was one of a pair of experimental engines built by Messrs Kerr Stuart in 1929 (works Nos 4421 and 4428), the first being a 0–6–0 and the second a 0–4–0. They were of standard 4ft 8½in gauge. The 0–6–0 commenced work on the Eskdale Railway, well known now as a narrow gauge system, but which at that time also had some standard gauge track serving a stone quarry. This view, taken in 1935, shows the engine at Ravenglass. The quarry ceased operation in 1953, and the engine was sold to the National Coal Board for use at Wingate Colliery, Durham. In 1968 it was disposed of to the Trent Valley Trading Estate, Lichfield, where it was still at

work in 1979, and it is understood to be scheduled for preservation. The four-coupled engine was donated by the Redland Group of Bedfordshire brickworks to the Quainton Railway Society, and is now at their premises at Quainton Road station.

Bagnall fireless locomotive 1932

Typical of a specialised type of fireless locomotive used to a small extent by industrial firms where the fire risk is exceedingly high. The orthodox boiler is replaced by a steam reservoir, charged with water and steam at a high pressure of something like 200lb per square inch, fed to the cylinders through a reducing valve until the working pressure drops below a practicable limit of about 80lb, when it has to be recharged. A locomotive of 2ft 6in gauge, works No 216 of 1923, is illustrated at Kemsley Mill in 1969. It is now preserved on the Sittingbourne and Kemsley Light Railway. Another engine was one of a pair owned by Messrs Huntley & Palmer of Reading, built by Bagnall in 1932. It is now owned by Mr J. Gretton and is on the West Somerset Railway. Other examples of fireless locomotives are to be found at Steamtown, Quainton Road and Swansea Industrial Museum (built by Barclay).

Ford Motor Co Ltd British Thomson-Houston diesel-electric shunter

1932

One of three early diesel-electric locomotives built in 1932 by British Thomson-Houston Ltd for the Ford Motor Co Ltd of Dagenham, Essex. Now acquired by the Kent & East Sussex Railway, Tenterden, Kent.

Beyer Peacock Garratt 0–4–4–0

1937

Driving wheels: 3ft 4in
Weight: 61 tons
Cylinders: (4) 13½in × 20in
Pressure: 180lb
Tractive effort: 24,600lb

The last Garratt engine to be built for use in this country, and the only standard gauge one

to be preserved here. It was built by Messrs Beyer Peacock & Company in 1937 (works No 6841) and worked at Baddesley Colliery, Warwick, until the year 1966. It was intended that it should go to Canada for preservation, but fortunately the deal fell through, and in 1968 it was purchased jointly by Mr J. Price and Mr Alan Bloom, and is now at the latter's museum

of preserved locomotives at Bressingham Hall, Diss, where it is sometimes steamed. It bears the name *William Francis*, is now painted in the yellow livery of the old Midland Great Northern Joint Railway and carries the makers' number, 6841, in large figures on each bunker.

R.Stephenson & Hawthorn crane tanks 0–4–0CT   1940

The Doxford Shipyard at Pallion, Sunderland, which closed early in 1971, had at that time still in use five 0–4–0T crane engines, of which four were secured for preservation. Four of the five were of a design introduced in 1940, in which year two engines were built by Messrs Robert Stephenson and Hawthorn (works Nos 7006 and 7007), named *Roker* and *Hendon*, followed by two more in 1942 (Nos 7069 and 7070), *Southwick* and *Millfield*. The last named was purchased by Mr J. Price (who was also instrumental in the preservation of the last Garratt) and is, like the Garratt, now housed at Bressingham Hall. *Southwick* has gone to Dinting, whilst *Roker*, is on the Foxfield Railway and *Hendon* on the Tanfield Railway.

Fairfield electric loco   1940

0–4–0 electric locomotive with overhead transmission, built in 1940 by the English Electric Company, Stafford, (works No 1131) for the Fairfield Shipbuilding Company, Govan, Glasgow. Now at the premises of the Railway Preservation Society, Falkirk.

Bagnall 0–4–0ST   1943

Driving wheels: 2ft 9in
Weight: 16¾ tons
Cylinders: 16in × 10in

Pressure: 160lb
Tractive effort: 6,140lb

Built by Bagnall of Stafford in 1943 (works No 2702). Supplied to Thomas Frith & Brown. Sold to J. Fraser & Co, Barnsley, who in turn disposed of it to Cohen's of Stanningley. Acquired by the Middleton Railway Trust in 1966 and now to be seen at their premises near Leeds, named *Matthew Murray*.

Sentinel shunters   1947

This engine is typical of several Sentinel engines which have been preserved, see further details on page 183. This particular one was owned by the Chesterfield Tube Company, it is preserved at the Lytham Motive Power Museum.

Barclay & Peckett 0—4—0STs

1948

Data: Barclay engine
Driving wheels: 3ft 2in
Weight: 22¼ tons
Cylinders: 12in×20in
Pressure: 160lb
Tractive effort: 10,307lb

Built by Andrew Barclay in 1946, their No 2226 was for ICI Ltd, for use at its dyestuffs works at Huddersfield, this engine was presented to the K&WVR in 1968. Two similar engines Nos 2220 and 2221, also built in 1946 for Chatham and Devonport Dockyards are now respectively on the Chasewater Railway and the Dowty Preservation Society's premises at Ashchurch. The other engine in the illustration is a Peckett works No 1999 of 1941, it went new to Southport gasworks, later being transferred to Darwen, where it worked until 1963. It was also acquired by the Keighley & Worth Valley Railway, but has since been removed to Southport.

Barclay 0—4—0ST

1948

A typical Barclay four-coupled saddle tank, built in large numbers for industrial use until the early 1950s, by which time steam was largely superseded by diesel replacements.

No 2248 of 1948 worked at the British Sugar Corporation's works at Wissington. Latterly owned by Mr Heugh, whose father was a driver at Barton shed and whose last journey

on a steam locomotive was on No 90432, which accounts for the adoption of this number in BR style on the smokebox door. The locomotive is on the Nene Valley Railway, Peterborough.

Barclay 0–4–0WT

1949

Driving wheels: 2ft 0in
Weight: 10¾ tons
Cylinders: 8½in × 12in
Pressure: 180lb
Gauge: 3ft 0in

Three engines built by Andrew Barclay in 1949 (works Nos 2263-2265) for Bord Na Mona (Irish Turf Board) for use on the peat bogs at Portarlington. No 1 has been purchased by the Talyllyn Railway for conversion to its gauge. No 2 has been acquired by the Irish Steam Preservation Society, Stradbally, and No 3, named *Shane*, now works on a pleasure railway at Shane's Castle, Antrim.

R. Stephenson & Hawthorn 0–4–0ST 'Bonnie Prince Charlie'

1949

Built by Robert Stephenson & Hawthorns in 1949 (works No 7544) for Corrall's Dibble Wharf, Northam, Southampton. Purchased in 1969 by the Salisbury Steam Locomotive Preservation Trust. Now housed at the Didcot Railway Centre.

161

R. Stephenson & Hawthorn 0–6–0T   1949

Driving wheels: 3ft 8in
Weight: 52¼ tons
Cylinders: 18in×24in
Pressure: 175lb
Tractive effort: 26,000lb

A powerful design of 0–6–0T for heavy shunting introduced by Messrs Robert Stephenson & Hawthorn in 1949. The first engine, works No 7597, is preserved on the Stour Valley Railway, and others are to be found on the North Yorkshire Moors Railway, the Shackerstone Society, and at Beamish Museum (see entries in the R. S. Hawthorn index). The one illustrated, No 7745 of 1952, built for the CEGB power station at Meaford, near Stoke-on-Trent, is on a preserved line in the USA, the Boyne City Railroad, Michigan, in bright green livery with British Railways emblem, although it was never a BR engine. It is known as No 22 *The Flying Duchess*. Others of this class that have been preserved include Nos 7845 and 7846, built in 1953 for the CEGB Hams Hall power station, now respectively on the North Norfolk Railway and at the Chappel Steam Centre.

Bagnall 0–4–4–0T 'Monarch'   1953

Driving wheels: 2ft
Weight: 28½ tons
Cylinders: (4) 9in × 12in
Pressure: 185lb
Tractive effort: 12,737lb

One of the few Mallett type engines ever to work in this country. Built by Bagnall's in 1953 (works No 3024) for Bowaters Lloyd Pulp and Paper Mills, Sittingbourne. In certain technical details the engine is not a true Mallett, which should have the rear power bogie rigid with the main frame, and should also ideally be a compound. A 'modified Meyer articulated engine' might be a better description. Purchased privately in 1966 and transferred to the Welshpool and Llanfair Preservation Society.

War Department Austerity 0–6–0ST 1941

Driving wheels: 4ft 1½in
Weight: 49.5 tons
Cylinders: 18in × 26in
Pressure: 170lb
Tractive effort: 26,280lb

In previous editions of this book these engines have been included in the 'main line' section, but it has now been found more appropriate to transfer them to the industrial pages, as so many of them built since the war for the NCB and similar organisations were never in service with the War Department. Their numbers have grown so much of recent years that they have now become the most numerous preserved class anywhere, even exceeding the Hunslet slate quarry engines. Their origin goes back to the 1930s with the Hunslet Engine Co, but may best be regarded as commencing with eight engines in 1941, known as the 50550 class, of which three actually ran as WD engines for a time.

Three of these Hunslet engines have survived:

Works No 2411 of 1941 Corby Steelworks No 24, preserved by the Corby & District Model Railway Club.
Works No 2413 of 1941 From the British Steel Corporation, Harlaston, now *Gunby* at the Chappel Steam Centre carrying the number 68067, not to be confused with LNER No 8067, one of the later true 'Austerities' WD No 71474.
Works No 2414 of 1941 Was WD No 70066, sold to the Port of London Authority, their No 79, then to Ackton Hall Colliery, and now preserved at Embsay, Yorkshire Dales Railway.

The true Austerities were introduced in 1943 by the Ministry of Supply for wartime duties.

Several hundred were built, and production continued after the war for general industrial use, some to a slightly modified design. The final one of all, turned out in 1964 for the Cadeby Main Colliery, and now to be seen at Quainton Road, achieved history in being the last standard gauge steam locomotive to be built for use in this country. After the war many of them were sold out of service to collieries and other industrial organisations, 75 of them were purchased by the LNER as Class J94, eventually becoming Nos 68006 to 68080.

The following is a summary, at the time of writing, of those which have been preserved, but there is still the possibility of others still in industrial use being added to the list, which contains locomotives based on the Austerity design.

Hunslet Engine Co: War Department locomotives

Works No	Built	WD No	Later owner	Preservation
2855	1943	75006	Onllwyn Colliery	Nene Valley Railway
2864	1943	75015	Backworth No 48	Strathspey Railway
2868	1943	75019/168	NCB Glasshoughton	MOIRA Leicester
2879	1943	75030	Whitwood Colliery	Brechin Railway Preservation Society
2890	1943	75041/107	Maesteg Colliery	Dart Valley Railway *Maureen*
3193	1944	75142/140	Chapeltown, Yorks	Midland Railway Centre

Robert Stephenson & Hawthorn: War Department locomotives

Works No	Built	WD No	Later owner	Preservation
7086	1943	75050	Long Marston	K&ESR
7097	1943	75061	Backworth No 9	Strathspey Railway
7098	1943	75062	Backworth No 49	Tanfield Railway
7136	1944	75186/150		Dinting Railway Centre *Warrington*
7169	1944	71515	Ashington Colliery	East Somerset Railway No 68005
7289	1945	71480	Manchester Collieries	K&WVR *Fred*

Andrew Barclay: War Department locomotives

Works No	Built	WD No	Later owner	Preservation
2215	1946	71466	LNER No 8077	K&WVR No 68077

William Bagnall & Sons: War Department locomotives

Works No	Built	WD No	Later owner	Preservation
2750	1944	75161/145		Bicester Ordnance Depot *The Storeman*
2759	1944	75171/147	Wemyss Private Railway No 16	Lochty Railway
2766	1944	75178	Treochy Colliery	Dart Valley Railway

Hudswell Clarke: War Department locomotives

Works No	Built	WD No	Later owner	Preservation
1776	1944	71499	Walkden Colliery	Chequerbent, Lancashire
1782	1945	71505/118		K&WVR No 118 *Brussels*

Vulcan Foundary: War Department locomotives

Works No	Built	WD No	Later owner	Preservation
5309	1945	75319	South Hetton No 12	Colne Valley Railway

Hunslet Engine Co: Postwar War department locomotives

3790	1952	WD 190/90		Colne Valley Railway
				Castle Hedingham
3791	1952	WD 191/91		K&ESR No 23
				Holmon F. Stephens
3792	1953	WD 192/92	*Waggoner*	Marchwood WD Depot
3793	1953	WD 193/93		Severn Valley Railway
				No 193 *Shropshire*
3794	1953	WD 194/94		L&HLR *Cumbria*
3796	1953	WD 196	*Errol Lonsdale*	Mid-Hants Railway
3797	1953	WD 197	*Sapper*	K&ESR
3798	1953	WD 198/98	*Royal Engineer*	Long Marsden WD Depot
3800	1953	WD 200/95		K&ESR No 24
				William H. Austin

Locomotives built new for the National Coal Board, and other industrial users.

Hunslet Engine Co: Postwar locomotives for industrial use

3686	1948	Dawson Colliery, Seaham Harbour	Strathspey Railway
3698	1950	NCB Walkden, *Repulse*	Lakeside & Haverthwaite Railway
3715	1952	Primrose Colliery, Yorkshire	Yorkshire Dales Railway
		Primrose No 2	
3777	1952	Wolstanton Colliery No 9	North Staffordshire Railway
3783	1953	Darfield Colliery No 1	Yorkshire Dales Railway
3785	1953	South Hetton No 69	Yorkshire Dales Railway
3806	1953	West Cannock No 4	Norchard Steam Centre
3810	1954	Hafodrynys Colliery *Glendower*	Dart Valley Railway
3839	1956	Cannock Wood No 7 *Wimblebury*	Foxfield Railway
3850	1958	Stewart & Lloyds, Buckminster	Quainton Road
3890*	1964	Cadeby Main Colliery	Quainton Road

*Last standard gauge engine built for use in this country.

Finally a slightly more powerful version of the class appeared in 1950 from the works of Robert Stephensons & Hawthorns, the principal difference in the dimensions being that the driving wheels were 4ft in place of the 4ft 3in, boiler pressure 180lb in lieu of 175lb, weight increased from 48 tons to 53 tons, and the wheelbase was extended from 9ft to 10ft. The main visual difference being that the saddle tank is shortened and does not extend back to cover the firebox fully.

Five of these engines survive:

7667	1950	Stewart & Lloyds, Corby No 56	K&ESR No 26
7668	1950	Stewart & Lloyds, Corby No 57	K&WVR *Samson*
7671	1950	Stewart & Lloyds, Corby No 60	Chappel Steam Centre
			Jupiter
7673	1950	Stewart & Lloyds, Corby No 62	K&WVR
7761	1954	Stewart & Lloyds, Corby No 63	K&WVR

Part Four

French 0–6–0T 'Cambrai'

1888

Driving wheels: (900mm) 2ft 1½in (the centre pair of wheels are flangeless)

Cylinders: (300mm × 450mm) 12in × 18in
Gauge: Metre

One of the very few French-built locomotives ever to work in this country. It was one of a pair built by Corpet et Louvet of Paris, this one in 1888 (works No 493). It was purchased by the Loddington Ironstone Co, Kettering, in 1936 and in 1956 was transferred to the Waltham Iron Co, Leicestershire, where it worked until the line was closed in 1959. It was presented to the Narrow Gauge Railway Museum Trust in 1960, and was on display at Towyn Museum, but has now been acquired by A. Keefe Ltd of Bampton for restoration to working order.

Danish 0–4–0WT

1895

Driving wheels: 3ft 7½in
Cylinder: 13in × 20in
Weight: 23.8 tons
Pressure: 140lb
Maximum speed: 16mph

Built by Hartmann (works No 2110) in 1895. From Odense, purchased by the Steam Power Trust (1965) Stockton-on-Tees for use on the Middleton Railway.

Oakbank Oil Company electric No 2

1902

Equipment: Two 25hp 500V traction motors by Westinghouse Electric Co
Collection: Overhead
Gauge: 2ft 6in

The second of two electric locomotives built in 1902 by the Baldwin Locomotive Co, Philadelphia, USA (works Nos 20586 and 20587)

for working between Niddry Castle Works, Winchburgh, Scotland and Duddingston Shale Mines. The line was closed in 1960 and the locomotive was presented by Scottish Oils Ltd, West Lothian to the Royal Scottish Museum, Edinburgh, where the engine now rests.

Beyer Peacock 0–4–4–0 Garratt compound

1909

Driving wheels: 2ft 7½in
Weight: 33½ tons
Cylinders: (2 high pressure) 11in × 26in (2 low pressure) 17in × 26in
Pressure: 195lb
Tractive effort: 16,290lb
Gauge: 2ft

The first Garratt locomotive constructed by Beyer Peacock & Co in 1909, forerunner of many other machines which that company built, chiefly for overseas railways, particularly South Africa and Rhodesia. This engine was for the Tasmanian Government Railways, 2ft gauge, and on withdrawal from service in 1947 was re-purchased by the makers and exhibited at their works, at Gorton, Manchester. The firm closed down in 1965, when the locomotive was acquired by the Festiniog Railway, who hoped to use it on their own line, but it has now gone to the National Railway Museum, York.

PLM (SNCF Class 231K) 4–6–2 No 231K22   1914

Driving wheels: 6ft 8½in
Weight: (engine only) 87 metric tons

From SNCF (Societé Nationale Chemin de Fer) French State Railways. Originally built in 1914 for the Paris Lyons Mediterranean Railway, rebuilt 1936. Became Nord 231K22. Now preserved at Steamtown, Carnforth.

Nordic 2–6–0   1919

Driving wheels: 4ft 7½in
Cylinders: 17in × 24in
Pressure: 170lb
Weight: (engine and tender) 61½ tons
Tractive effort: 18,058lb

The last of a series of 70 handsome 2–6–0s built for the Norwegian railways from the 1880s. The first three were built by Messrs Dübs and Company of Glasgow, and the design was credited to David Jones of the Highland Railway. The last eight, known as the Class 21C, appeared in 1919 from the firm of Nydquist and Han. No 377 was purchased in 1971 by Mr and Mrs G. Pagano, and brought to England, stored for a time temporarily at Bressingham Hall, and later at Quainton Road; it is now owned by Mr and Mrs Tony Parker and works on the CGR Main Line Steam Trust at Loughborough. It is painted in apple green livery and bears the name *King Haakon 7*. A similar engine, No 376, is at Tenterden on the Kent & East Sussex Railway.

Baguley 0–4–0T 'Rishra'   1921

Driving wheels: 1ft 3½in
Cylinders: 4in × 8in
Pressure: 150lb
Weight: 3½ tons
Gauge: 2ft

The second of two locomotives built by Baguley and Company in 1921 (works No 2006 and 2007). Shipped to India in 1922 for use hauling coal on a line from a wharf on the Hoogly River to Calcutta works pumping station at Barrakpore, near Calcutta. Discovered lying derelict in 1963 by Mr M. Satow, the present owner, restored to working order at Rishra works, and shipped back to England in 1971. Now at work on the Leighton Buzzard Light Railway under the name of *Rishra*.

Romney Hythe & Dymchurch 0–4–0
No 4 'The Bug'   1926

Driving wheels: 15¾in
Weight: 5 tons
Cylinders: 4½in × 6¼in
Pressure: 170lb
Gauge: 1ft 3in

Built by Krauss of Munich in 1926 (works No 8738) for the RH&DR, No 4 *The Bug*. Sold 1933 to Belfast Corporation Tramways, later used in pleasure park. Retrieved from a scrapyard in Belfast in 1972 and brought back to New Romney for preservation. It has since been rebuilt and is steamed on special occasions only.

Krupp 4–6–2   1937

Driving wheels: 6in × 14½in
Weight: 8½ tons
Pressure: 200lb
Gauge: 1ft 3in

Two narrow-gauge Pacifics are working on the miniature Waveney Valley Railway at Bressingham Steam Museum, the creation of Alan Bloom, of Bressingham Hall, Diss, Norfolk. Built by Krupps of Essen in 1937 (works Nos 1662 and 1663), they are *Rosenkavalier* and *Mannertreu*. They first ran at an exhibition at Dusseldorf in 1937, after which they appear to have been stored, no doubt throughout the war. They reappeared at another exhibition at Cologne in 1952, after which they were again laid up for many years before being brought over to this country by Mr Bloom. A third example, (works No 1664) is now on the Romney, Hythe and Dymchurch Railway as their No 11 *Black Prince*.

US Army 2–8–0   1942

Driving wheels: 4ft 9in
Weight: 124 tons
Cylinders: 19in × 26in
Pressure: 225lb
Tractive effort: 31,490lb

Introduced in 1942 by the US Army Transportation Corps for service in Western Europe. Several hundred were built by the American Locomotive Company; Baldwin Locomotive Company and the Lima Locomotive Company. Many were loaned to this country during 1943 and 1944 and were to be seen on the main lines of the LMS, LNER and GWR. This particular example was one of a postwar batch built by Lima in 1945 (works No 8758) for the Polish State Railways, their No 203.474 (originally No 5820). It was imported from Poland by the Keighly & Worth Valley Railway who have temporary repainted it in grey livery with the number 2820.

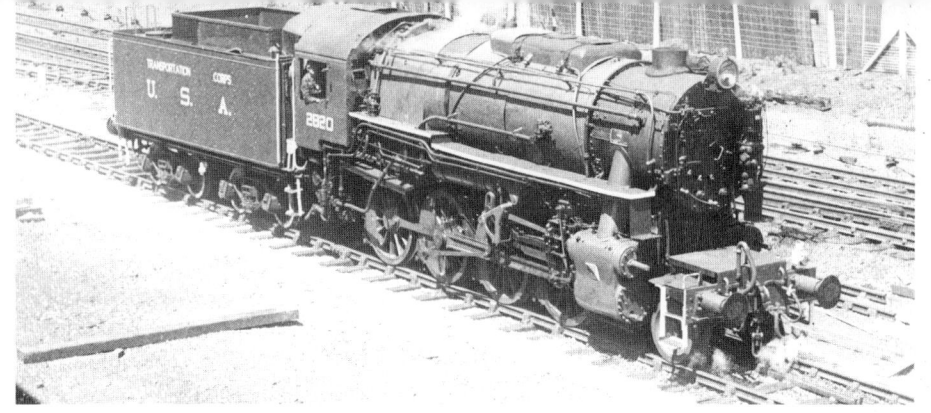

Austrian 0–8–0T No 10 'Sir Drefaldwyn'   1944

Gauge: 2ft 6in

Built by Societe Franco-Belges Raismes, in 1944 (work No 2855) for Deutsche Heeresfeldbahnen. Sold 1946 to Salzkammergut Lokalbahn and again to Steirmarkische Landesbahnen (Styrian Provincial Railway) in 1958, on which railway it became No 699–01. Brought to Wales in 1969 for use on the Welshpool and Llanfair Light Railway, and now known as No 10 *Sir Drefaldwyn*.

Swedish State 2–6–4T No 1928   1953

Driving wheels: 4ft 7in
Weight: 78 tons
Cylinders: (2) 18½in×24in
Pressure: 160lb

A 2–6–4T imported from Sweden by the Peterborough Railway Society Ltd, now known as the Nene Valley Railway. No 1928, Swedish State Railways, Class SJ, was built by Nydqvist och Holm AB in 1953 and is oil-fired, using diesel oil.

Index of Industrial and Light Railways' Locomotives

This summary of industrial and light railways' locomotives is listed under private manufacturers in alphabetical order, embracing all known industrial steam locomotives at the time of compilation. The following abbreviations are used:

CSPS	Cornish Steam Preservation Society	NGC	Narrow Gauge Centre, Blaenau Ffestiniog
GCR/MLST	Great Central Railway/Main Line Steam Trust	NYMR	North Yorkshire Moors Railway
ISPS	Irish Steam Preservation Society	R&ER	Ravenglass & Eskdale Railway
		RH&DR	Romney, Hythe & Dymchurch Railway
K&WVR	Keighley & Worth Valley Railway	RPSI	Railway Preservation Society of Ireland
K&ESR	Kent & East Sussex Railway		
L&HLR	Lakeside & Haverthwaite Light Railway	S&KLR	Sittingbourne & Kemsley Light Railway
LBLR	Leighton Buzzard Light Railway	W&LLR	Welshpool and Llanfair Light Railway

Aveling and Porter Ltd, Rochester

Works No.	Year	Wheel Argt.	Name	Location
807	1872	0–4–0WT		London Transport Museum
1607	1880	2–2–0WT	Excelsior	Castle Donington
3567	1895	0–4–0WT	Sydenham	Quainton Road
6158	1906	0–4–0WT	Sirapite	Steamtown, Carnforth
8800	1917	0–4–0WT	Sir Vincent	Hollycombe Woodland Railway
9449	1926	2–2–0WT	Blue Circle	Bluebell Railway

Avonside Engine Co Ltd, Bristol

1386	1897	0–6–0ST	Trojan	Didcot Railway Centre
1421	1900	0–6–0ST	Pontyberem	Didcot Railway Centre
1465	1908	0–4–0ST		Liverpool Museum
1498	1906	0–4–0ST	Desmond	Caerphilly Railway Society
1547	1908	0–6–0T	Nancy	Shane's Castle (3ft gauge)
1568	1909	0–6–0ST	Lucy	Steamport, Southport
1572	1910	0–6–0ST	Woolmer	National Railway Museum
1720	1915	0–4–0T	Sezela No 2	Great Bush Railway (2ft gauge)
1738	1916	0–4–0T	Sezela No 4	Knebworth Park (2ft gauge)
1748	1916	0–4–0T	Woolwich	Bicton Woodland Railway (1ft 6in) gauge)
1764	1917	0–6–0ST	Portbury	West Somerset Railway
1772	1917	0–4–0ST	Asklam Hall	L&HLR
1798	1918	0–6–0ST	Edwin Hulse	Bristol Suburban Railway
1800	1918	0–6–0ST	Percy	In store
1810	1918	0–6–0ST		Skelmersdale New Town
1865	1922	0–4–0ST	Elizabeth	W. H. McAlpine
1875	1921	0–4–0ST	Barrington	Colne Valley Railway
1883	1922	0–6–0ST	1833	Dinting Railway Centre
1908	1925	0–4–0ST	Fred	Nene Valley Railway
1917	1924	0–6–0ST	Pitsford	Nene Valley Railway
1919	1924	0–6–0ST	Cranford	Foxfield Light Railway
1928	1923	0–4–0T	Sezela No 6	Great Bush Railway (2ft gauge)
1945	1926	0–6–0ST		Nene Valley Railway
1972	1927	0–6–0ST	Stamford	Bluebell Railway
1973	1927	0–4–0DT	Dora	Market Overton
1977	1972	0–4–0WT	Cadbury No 1	Dowty RPS
2021	1928	0–6–0ST	No 3 R. H. Smyth	RPSI (5ft 3in gauge)
2057	1931	0–4–4–0TG	Renishaw No 4	W. Lees, Farncombe (2ft gauge)

2066	1933	0–4–0T	Ogwen	In the USA
2u67	1933	0–4–0T	Marchlyn	In the USA
2068	1933	0–6–0ST	Robert	Foxfield Light Railway
2071	1933	0–4–0T	Elidir	In Canada

W. G. Bagnall Ltd, Stafford

1484	1898	2–4–0T	Sea Lion	Groudle Glen, IOM (1ft 11½in gauge)
1491	1897	0–4–0ST	Isabel	Stafford station (2ft gauge)
1568	1899	0–4–0ST	Dorothy	NGC Blaenau Ffestiniog (2ft gauge)
1760	1906	0–4–0ST	Sybil	J. J. A. Evans Launceston (1ft 10¾in gauge)
1781	1908	2–4–0T	Polar Bear	Brockham Museum (1ft 11½in gauge)
1877	1918	0–6–2T	Chevallier	Whipsnade Park (2ft 6in gauge)
1889	1911	0–4–0ST		In store (3ft gauge)
2043	1917	0–4–0ST	Kidbrooke	In store (1ft 11½in gauge)
2067	1917	0–4–0ST	Peter	Brockham Museum Trust (1ft 11½in gauge)
2087	1918	0–4–0ST	Leonard	Birmingham Science Museum (2ft gauge)
2088	1918	0–4–0ST	Lady Luxborough	Mr D. A. Smith, Warwickshire (2ft gauge)
2090	1919	0–4–0ST	Pixie	Cadeby Light Railway (2ft gauge)
2091	1919	0–4–0ST	Wendy	Hampshire Narrow Gauge Railway Society (2ft gauge)
2128	1921	0–4–0ST	No 2	Yorkshire Dales Railway
2133	1924	0–4–0ST	Woto	Romford, Essex (3ft 6½in gauge)
2135	1925	0–4–0ST	Sir Tom	Romford, Essex (3ft 6½in gauge)
2192	1922	0–6–2T	Conqueror	Whipsnade Zoo (2ft 6in gauge)
2193	1922	0–4–0WT	Topham	Foxfield Light Railway
2216	1923	2–4–0F	Unique	S&KLR (2ft 6in gauge)
2221	1927	0–6–0ST	Lewisham	Foxfield Light Railway
2450	1931	0–4–0ST	J. T. Daly	Foxfield Light Railway
2469	1932	0–4–0ST	Scott	Quainton Road
2472	1932	0–6–2T	Alpha	S&KLR (2ft 6in gauge)
2473	1932	0–4–0F		West Somerset Railway
2511	1934	0–6–2T	Triumph	S&KLR (2ft 6in gauge)
2542	1936	0–4–0ST	Jubilee	Chappel Steam Centre
2545	1936	0–4–4–0TG	Renishaw 5	W. Lees, Farncombe (2ft gauge)
2565	1936	0–4–0ST		J. N. Walker, Witney
2572	1937	0–4–0ST	Judy	St Austell Industrial Museum
2623	1940	0–4–0ST	Hawarden	Foxfield Light Railway
2624	1940	0–6–2T	Superb	S&KLR (2ft 6in gauge)
2648	1941	0–4–0ST	Dunlop No 6	Market Bosworth Light Railway
2654	1942	0–6–0ST	Cherwell	Daventry Recreation Ground
2655	1942	0–6–0ST	Huntsman	Hunt & Co, Hinckley
2668	1942	0–6–0ST	Cranford No 2	Steamtown Carnforth
2670	1942	0–6–0ST	Lamport No 3	GCR/MLST
2680	1944	0–6–0ST	No 4	North Norfolk Railway
2682	1942	0–6–0ST	Princess	L&HLR
2692	1942	0–4–0ST		CSPS
2702	1943	0–4–0ST	Mathew Murray	Middleton Railway
2749	1944	0–6–0ST		Brechin Railway Preservation Society
2750	1944	0–6–0ST	Storeman	Bicester Ordnance Depot
2759	1944	0–6–0ST	No 16	Lochty Railway
2766	1944	0–6–0ST		Dart Valley Railway
2820	1946	4–4–0T	No 23 Isibutu	Knebworth Park (2ft gauge)

Works No.	Year	Wheel Argt.	Name	Location
2842	1946	0–4–0ST	No 2	Mid-Hants Railway
2895	1948	0–4–2T		P. Rampton, Loxhill
2962	1950	0–4–0ST		Didcot Railway Centre
2994	1950	0–6–0ST	Vulcan	West Somerset Railway
2996	1950	0–6–0ST	Victor	West Somerset Railway
3019	1952	0–6–0F	Trimpell	Steamtown, Carnforth
3024	1953	0–4–4–0T	Monarch	W&LLR (2ft 6in gauge)
3058	1953	0–4–0ST	Alfred	CSPS
3059	1953	0–6–0ST	Florence No 2	Market Bosworth Light Railway
3090	1956	2–6–2T	Campbell	J. Hurst & Son, Andover (2ft 0¼in gauge)
3121	1957	0–4–0F		CSPS

E. E. Baguley Ltd, Burton-on-Trent

Works No.	Year	Wheel Argt.	Name	Location
646	1917	0–4–0P		R. Morris, Longfield (2ft gauge)
680	1916	0–4–0P	Jacob	Dinting Railway Centre
736	1918	0–4–0P		R. Morris, Longfield (2ft gauge)
760	1918	0–4–0P		R. Morris, Longfield (2ft gauge)
774	1919	0–4–0P		B. W. Goodchild, Leamington Spa (2ft gauge)
800	1920	0–4–0P		Shugborough Museum
1695	1928	0–4–0P		Cadeby Light Railway (2ft gauge)
2007	1921	0–4–0T	Rishra	LBLR (2ft gauge)

Andrew Barclay & Sons, Kilmarnock

Works No.	Year	Wheel Argt.	Name	Location
699	1891	0–4–0ST	Swanscombe	Quainton Road
776	1896	0–4–0ST	Punch Hull	Quainton Road
782	1896	0–6–0ST	Peter	Ironbridge Gorge Museum
807	1887	0–4–0ST	Bon Accord	Aberdeen City Council
840	1899	0–4–0T	Borrowstournness	SRPS, Falkirk (3ft gauge)
880	1902	0–4–0CT	Glenfield No 1	Steamtown, Carnforth
885	1902	0–4–0ST	No 8	Cambrian Railway Society
929	1902	0–4–0ST	Alexandra	L&HLR
945	1904	0–4–0ST	No 945	Bury Transport Museum
984	1903	0–4–0WT	No 3	NGC Blaenau Ffestiniog (2ft 6in gauge)
988	1903	0–4–0WT	No 5	Clerminster Museum (2ft gauge)
1015	1904	0–6–0ST	No 1 Horden	Tanfield Railway
1047	1905	0–4–0ST	No 1047	Chappel Steam Centre
1081	1909	0–4–0ST	Leaf	John Player & Sons, Clydach-on-Tawe
1147	1908	0–4–0ST	No 5 John Howe	Steamtown, Carnforth
1193	1910	0–4–0ST	No 6	Tanfield Railway
1219	1910	0–4–0ST		South Cambridgeshire Museum
1223	1911	0–4–0ST		Chasewater Light Railway
1260	1911	0–4–0ST	Forester	Caerphilly Railway Society
1385	1914	0–4–0ST	Rosyth No 1	Swansea Museum
1398	1915	0–4–0ST	Lord Fisher	East Somerset Railway
1431	1918	0–4–0WT	No 6 Douglas	Talyllyn Railway (2ft 3in gauge)
1458	1916	0–6–0ST		SRPS, Falkirk
1473	1916	0–4–0F	Sir Charles	Swansea Museum
1477	1916	0–4–0F	GF3	Quainton Road
1571	1917	0–6–0F	No 1	Glasgow Museum
1578	1918	0–6–0T	Gertrude	Welsh Highland Light Railway (2ft gauge)
1598	1918	0–4–0ST	Efficient	Steamport, Southport

1605	1918	0–6–0T	Ajax	Isle of Wight Steam Centre
1641	1918	0–6–0T	The Doll	LBLR (2ft gauge)
1659	1920	0–4–0ST	No 32	Tanfield Railway
1791	1930	0–4–0ST	Glenfield	East Somerset Railway
1815	1924	0–4–0F	No 2	Leicester Museum
1833	1924	0–6–0ST	Alexander	Strathspey Railway
1865	1925	0–4–0ST	No 6	Quainton Road
1871	1925	0–4–0WT		Eddleston (2ft 6in gauge)
1875	1925	0–4–0CT	Stanton No 24	Midland Railway Centre
1876	1925	0–6–0F		S&KLR (2ft 6in gauge)
1890	1927	0–4–0WT	No 10 Forth	Strathspey Railway
1927	1927	0–4–0ST	No 1	Bury Transport Museum
1931	1927	0–4–0ST		Market Overton
1932	1927	0–4–0ST		Buckminster Trust Estate
1937	1928	0–4–0ST	No 3	SRPS, Falkirk
1944	1931	0–6–0WT	Glyder	In the USA (1ft 11½in gauge)
1969	1929	0–4–0ST	Jane Darbyshire	Steamtown, Carnforth
1984	1930	0–4–0F	No 1	Foxfield Light Railway
1991	1931	0–4–0ST	Cegin	In the USA (1ft 11½in gauge)
1995	1931	0–4–0WT	No 7 Caledonia	Hollycombe Woodland Railway (2ft gauge)
1996	1931	0–6–0ST	Victor	West Somerset Railway
2015	1935	0–4–0ST	Tom Parry	Quainton Road
2017	1935	0–6–0T	No 7	Strathspey Railway
2020	1936	0–4–0ST	No 2 Balmenach	Strathspey Railway
2046	1937	0–4–0ST	No 3	Chasewater Light Railway
2047	1937	0–6–0ST		Strathspey Railway
2068	1939	0–6–0ST	No 1 Dalurine	SRPS, Falkirk
2073	1939	0–6–0ST	Daluaine	Strathspey Railway
2086	1940	0–4–0ST	Drake	Dowty RPS
2088	1940	0–4–0ST	Sir Thomas Royden	Market Overton
2107	1941	0–6–0T	Harlaxton	North Norfolk Railway
2126	1942	0–4–0F		Dowty RPS
2134	1942	0–4–0ST	Coronation	Steamtown, Carnforth
2139	1942	0–6–0ST	Salmon	NYMR
2157	1942	0–4–0ST	No 47	SRPS, Falkirk
2199	1945	0–4–0ST	No 8 Victory	Colne Valley Railway
2201	1948	0–4–0ST	Victory	Caerphilly Railway Society
2207	1946	0–4–0WT	Dougal	W&LLR (2ft 6in gauge)
2215	1946	0–6–0ST	No 68077	K&WVR
2217	1947	0–4–0ST	Henry Ellison	In store
2219	1947	0–4–0ST	No 17	SRPS, Falkirk
2220	1946	0–4–0ST	Invicta	Chasewater Light Railway
2221	1946	0–4–0ST	No 2	Dowty RPS
2226	1946	0–4–0ST		K&WVR
2230	1947	0–4–0ST	No 1 Douglas	Steamtown, Carnforth
2239	1947	0–4–0ST	Mr Therm	In store
2243	1948	0–4–0F		Quainton Road
2248	1948	0–4–0ST	No 90432	Nene Valley Railway
2258	1949	0–4–0ST	Tiny	Dinting Railway Centre
2263	1949	0–4–0WT	No 7 Irish Pete	Talyllyn Railway (2ft 3in gauge)
2264	1949	0–4–0WT	No 2	Shanes Castle (3ft gauge)
2265	1949	0–4–0WT	Shane	Shanes Castle (3ft gauge)
2274	1949	0–4–0ST	No 22	Bowes Railway
2315	1951	0–4–0ST	Clyde	Strathspey Railway
2320	1952	0–4–0ST	No 22	Yorkshire Dales Railway
2323	1952	0–4–0ST		Wickstead Park, Kettering
2333	1953	0–4–0ST	David	L&HLR

Works No.	Year	Wheel Argt.	Name	Location
2243	1953	0–4–0ST		Steamtown Carnforth
2350	1953	0–6–0ST	*Belvoir*	Colne Valley Railway
2352	1954	0–4–0ST	*Richard Trevithick*	Swanage Railway
2372	1956	0–4–0F	No 1 *Imperial*	National Railway Museum

Bellis & Seekings

	1874		*Secondus*	Birmingham Science Museum (2ft 8in gauge)

Beyer Peacock & Co, Manchester

1827	1879	0–4–0ST	No 1872	Cambrian Railways Society
2464	1885	0–4–0	Tram engine	Tramway Museum, Crich
2734	1886	0–4–0	Tram engine	Dinting Railway Centre
2817	1887	0–4–0WT	*Dot*	Narrow Gauge Museum, Talyllyn (1ft 6in gauge)
3496	1903	0–6–0T	*The Earl*	W&LLR (2ft 6in gauge)
3497	1903	0–6–0T	*The Countess*	W&LLR (2ft 6in gauge)
5292	1909	0–4–4–0		National Railway Museum
6841	1937	0–4–4–0	No 6841	Bressingham

Black Hawthorn & Co, Gateshead

266	1873	0–4–0ST	*Holwell No 3*	Tanfield Railway
305	1874	0–4–0ST	*Bauxite*	Science Museum, Kensington
859	1885	0–4–0ST	*Kettering Furnaces No 3*	Penrhyn Castle Museum
912	1887	0–4–0ST	*City of Aberdeen*	SRPS, Falkirk

Borrows & Sons Ltd, St Helens

37	1898	0–4–0WT		NYMR
48	1906	0–4–0WT	*The King*	Market Bosworth Light Railway
53	1909	0–4–0WT	*Windle*	Middleton Railway

Brush Electrical Engineering Co, Loughborough

314	1906	0–4–0ST		Abbey Pumping Station, Leicester

Clarkson & Co Ltd, York

4669	1966	2–8–2	No 9 *River Mite*	Ravenglas & Eskdale Railway (1ft 3in gauge)

Coalbrookdale

	1865	0–4–0ST	No 5	Telford Steam Trust

Dubs & Co, Glasgow

2178	1885	0–6–0T	*Caledonia*	Port Erin Museum, IOM
2890	1892	0–6–2T	*West Clare* No 5	Ennis, Ireland
4101	1901	0–4–0CT		East Somerset Railway

George England & Co, New Cross, London

	1857	0–4–0WT	*Shannon*	Didcot Railway Centre
	1863	0–4–0STT	*Princess*	Festiniog Railway (1ft 11½in gauge)
	1863	0–4–0STT	*Prince*	Festiniog Railway (1ft 11½in gauge)
	1864	0–4–0STT	*Palmerston*	Draycott-in-the-Clay, Staffs (1ft 11½in gauge)
	1867	0–4–0STT	*Welsh Pony*	Festiniog Railway (1ft 11½in gauge)

English Electric Ltd, Stafford

717	1927	4WE		Tramway Museum Crich

1131	1940	4WE		SRPS, Falkirk
2007	1955	Co-Co	*Deltic*	Science Museum, Kensington
2345	1956	0–6–0DE	No D0226	K&WVR

Falcon Engineering Works, Loughborough (incorporated into Brush Electric)

| 323 | 1878 | 0–4–0ST | No 3 | Talyllyn Railway (2ft 3in gauge) |

Fletcher Jennings & Co, Whitehaven

42	1865	0–4–0ST	No 1 *Talyllyn*	Talyllyn Railway (2ft 3in gauge)
63	1866	0–4–0WT	No 2 *Dolgoch*	Talyllyn Railway (2ft 3in gauge)
158	1877	0–4–0T	No 3 *Baxter*	Bluebell Railway
172	1880	0–4–0F	No 4	Brockham Museum (3ft 2¼in gauge)
173	1880	0–4–0T	No 5	J. B. Latham, Woking (3ft 2¼in gauge)

Fox Walker & Co, Atlas Works, Bristol

242	1874	0–6–0ST		Bristol Industrial Museum
385	1878	0–6–0ST	*Minnie*	K&ESR
410	1878	0–6–0ST	*Margaret*	County Museum, Pembroke

Gibbs & Hogg, Airdrie

| | 1898 | 0–4–0T | NCB No 11 | Pittencrieff Park, Dunfermline |

Grant Ritchie & Co

| 272 | 1894 | 0–4–0ST | No 16 | Glenrothes District Council |
| 536 | 1914 | 0–4–2ST | No 17 | Scottish Industrial Preservation Society, Preston Park |

T. Green & Sons, Leeds

| 441 | 1908 | 0–6–2ST | | In store for Leeds Museum (2ft gauge) |

Hawthorn Leslie & Co, Newcastle-on-Tyne

2450	1899	0–4–0ST	*Albert*	Hollycombe Woodland Railway (1ft 11½in gauge)
2491	1901	0–4–0ST	*Henry*	Courtaulds, Coventry
2711	1907	0–4–0ST	*Cyclops*	Tanfield Railway
2780	1909	0–4–0ST	*Asbestos*	Chasewater Light Railway
2800	1909	0–4–0ST	*Met*	North Road Station, Darlington
2859	1911	0–4–0ST	No 2	Tanfield Railway
2918	1912	0–4–0ST	*Pony*	North Norfolk Railway
3056	1914	0–4–0ST	No 14	North of England Museum, Beamish
3135	1915	0–4–0ST	*Vectis*	Isle of Wight Loco Society, Haven Street
3240	1917	0–4–0ST	*Beatty*	Gables Service Station, Rayleigh
3437	1919	0–6–0ST	*Isabel*	West Somerset Railway
3513	1923	0–6–0ST	*Stagshaw*	Tanfield Railway
3581	1924	0–4–0ST	No 3	GCR/MLST
3715	1928	0–4–0ST	No 1	Colne Valley Railway
3717	1928	0–4–0ST	No 3	Quainton Road
3718	1928	0–4–0ST	*Swanscombe*	S&KLR
3721	1928	0–4–0ST	*Ettrick*	Burton-on-Trent Historical Society
3732	1932	0–4–0ST	*Faraday*	M. Bamford, Ashchurch
3799	1935	0–4–0ST	No 3 *Penicuik*	Lytham Motive Power Museum
3827	1934	0–6–0ST		Corby UDC
3829	1934	0–4–0F		Titanic Steamship Co, Ellastone
3835	1934	0–6–0ST	No 16	Nene Valley Railway
3860	1935	0–4–0ST	No 6	Middleton Railway
3865	1936	0–4–0ST	*Singapore*	Market Overton
3931	1938	0–6–0ST	No 21	Market Bosworth Light Railway

Works No.	Year	Wheel Argt.	Name	Location
Hawthorn's of Leith				
244	1861	0–4–0WT	*Ellesmere*	SRPS, Falkirk
Haydock Foundary, Haydock, Lancs				
C	1874	0–6–0WT	*Bellerophon*	K&WVR
Head Wrightson & Co, Thornaby-on-Tees				
21	1870	0–4–0VBT	No 27	Preston Park and Museum, Teeside
	1871	0–4–0VBT		North of England Museum, Beamish
33	1873	0–4–0VBT	No 17	Darlington North Road Museum
Robert Heath				
	1896	0–4–0ST		Shugborough Museum
F. C. Hibberd, Park Royal				
	1926	0–4–0DM		Chasewater Light Railway
	1929	0–4–0DM		Chasewater Light Railway
A. Horlock, Northfleet Ironworks, Kent				
	1848	0–4–0	*Fire Queen*	Penrhyn Castle Museum (4ft gauge)
Hudswell Clarke & Co Ltd, Leeds				
402	1893	0–4–0ST	*Lord Mayor*	K&WVR
431	1895	0–6–0ST	No 15	Chasewater Light Railway
526	1899	0–6–0T	*Hawarden*	Penrhyn Castle Museum
544	1900	0–6–0ST		National Museum of Wales, Cardiff
555	1901	0–4–0ST	No 813	Severn Valley Railway
573	1900	0–6–0ST	*Handyman*	Midland Railway Centre (3ft gauge)
633	1902	0–6–0ST	*Lord Granby*	In store for Leeds Museum (3ft gauge)
639	1902	0–4–2ST	*San Justo*	J. J. Evans, Launceston (1ft 10¾in gauge)
640	1902	0–4–0ST	*Santa Ana*	J. J. Evans, Launceston (1ft 10¾in gauge)
679	1903	0–6–0T	No 31 *Hamburg*	K&WVR
680	1903	0–6–0T	No 32 *Gothenburg*	Bury Transport Museum
750	1906	0–4–0ST	*Waleswood*	Steamport, Southport
1026	1913	0–6–0ST	No 31	W. H. McAlpine, Fawley
1152	1919	0–4–0ST	No 3 *Guinness*	RPSI (5ft 3in gauge)
1223	1916	0–6–0T	*Vesta*	Penrhyn Castle Museum
1243	1917	0–6–0ST	*Richboro*	Llangollen Railway Society
1308	1918	0–6–0T	*Rhos*	A. B. Mason, Burnham Market
1309	1917	0–4–0ST	*Henry de Lacy*	Middleton Railway
1316	1919	0–6–0ST		L&HLR
1334	1918	0–6–0T	*Sir Thomas*	Quainton Road
1366	1919	0–6–0ST	*Renishaw Ironworks No 6*	L&HLR
1369	1922	0–4–0ST	*Nellie*	Yorkshire Dales Railway
1397	1919	0–6–0T	No 67	K&WVR
1450	1922	0–6–0ST	No 8 *Dorothy*	Yorkshire Dales Railway
1464	1921	0–6–0T	No 70	Bury Transport Museum
1539	1924	0–6–0ST	*Derek Crouch*	Nene Valley Railway
1544	1924	0–6–0ST	No 3	Mid-Hants Railway
1604	1928	0–6–0ST		Nene Valley Railway
1631	1929	0–6–0ST	No 5	L&HLR
1643	1930	0–6–0WT	*Bronllwyd*	Bressingham (1ft 11½in gauge)
1661	1936	0–4–0ST		Lytham Motive Power Museum

1672	1937	0–4–0ST	*Irwell*	Tanfield Railway
1682	1937	0–6–0ST	*Julia*	Newark Folk Museum
1689	1937	0–4–0ST		Hallamshire Railway Society, Sheffield
1700	1938	0–6–0ST	*Wissington*	North Norfolk Railway
1704	1938	0–6–0T	*Nunlow*	Dinting Railway Centre
1709	1939	0–6–0ST	*Slough Estates No 5*	Yorkshire Dales Railway
1731	1942	0–6–0T		NYMR
1742	1943	0–4–0ST	*Millom*	Quainton Road
1776	1944	0–6–0ST		Chequerbent, Lancs
1782	1945	0–6–0ST	No 118 *Brussels*	K&WVR
1800	1947	0–6–0T	*Thomas*	Nene Valley Railway
1821	1948	0–6–0ST	140	Yorkshire Dales Railway
1822	1949	0–6–0ST	No S110	Chasewater Light Railway
1823	1949	0–6–0T		North of England Museum, Beamish
1857	1952	0–6–0T	No 2 *North Gawber*	Market Bosworth Light Railway
1864	1942	0–6–0T	*Firefly*	Steamtown, Carnforth
1882	1955	0–4–0ST	*Mirvale*	NYMR
1892	1961	0–6–0ST	No 4	Titanic Steamship Co, Ellastone

Hughes & Co

323	1878	0–4–2ST	No 3 *Sir Haydn*	Talyllyn Railway (2ft 3in gauge)

Hunslet Engine Co, Leeds

283	1882	0–4–0ST	*Charles*	Penrhyn Castle Museum (1ft 11½in gauge)
287	1882	0–4–0ST ·	*Trym*	Quainton Road
299	1882	0–6–0ST		Hunslet, Leeds
316	1883	0–4–0ST	*Gwynnedd*	Bressingham (1ft 11½in gauge)
317	1883	0–4–0ST	*Lilian*	Guildford (60cm gauge)
364	1885	0–4–0ST	*Winifred*	C. B. Annette, Tennessee, USA (1ft 10¾in gauge)
409	1886	0–4–0ST	*Velinheli*	J. J. Evans, Launceston (1ft 10¾in gauge)
469	1888	0–6–0ST	No 15 *Hastings*	K&ESR
492	1889	0–4–0ST	*King of the Scarlets*	Ontario, Canada (1ft 10¾in gauge)
493	1889	0–4–0ST	*Elidir*	Llanberis Lake Railway (1ft 11½in gauge)
541	1891	0–4–0ST	*Rough Pup*	Narrow Gauge Museum, Tywyn (1ft 10¾ in gauge)
542	1891	0–4–0ST	*Cloister*	Hampshire Narrow Gauge Society (1ft 11½in gauge)
554	1891	0–4–0ST	*Lilla*	J. B. Latham, Woking (1ft 11½in gauge)
555	1891	2–6–2T	No 5	Steamtown, Vermont, USA (3ft gauge)
589	1893	0–4–0ST	*Blanche*	Festiniog Railway (now 2–4–0STT) (1ft 11½in gauge)
590	1893	0–4–0ST	*Linda*	Festiniog Railway (now 2–4–0STT) (1ft 11½in gauge)
605	1894	0–4–0ST	*Margaret*	Cadeby Light Railway (2ft gauge)
606	1894	0–4–0ST	*Alan George*	Howden Clough Light Railway, Leeds (1ft 11½in gauge)
638	1895	0–4–0ST	*Jerry M*	J. M. Baldock, Liphook (2ft gauge)
671	1898	0–4–0ST	*Cackler*	Steam Organ Museum, Thursford (2ft gauge)
678	1898	0–4–0ST	*Bernstein*	Lytham Creek Railway (1ft 10¾in gauge)

Works No.	Year	Wheel Argt.	Name	Location
679	1898	0–4–0ST	Covercoat	J. L. Butler, Ripley (1ft 10¾in gauge)
680	1898	0–4–0ST	George B	Dowty RPS (1ft 10¾in gauge)
684	1898	0–4–0WT	Jack	In store for Leeds Museum (1ft 6in gauge)
686	1898	0–6–0T	The Lady Armaghdale	Severn Valley Railway
704	1899	0–4–0ST	Nesta	C. B. Annett, Tennessee, USA (1ft 10¾in gauge)
705	1899	0–4–0ST	Elin	Lincolnshire Coast Railway (60cm gauge)
707	1899	0–4–0ST	Britomart	Festiniog Railway (1ft 11½in gauge)
763	1901	0–4–0ST	Dorothea	Brecon Mountain Railway (2ft gauge)
779	1902	0–4–0ST	Holy War	Bala Lake Railway (1ft 11½in gauge)
780	1902	0–4–0ST	Alice	Bala Lake Railway (parts only) (1ft 11½in gauge)
822	1903	0–4–0ST	Maid Marion	Bala Lake Railway (1ft 11½in gauge)
823	1903	0–4–0ST	Irish Mail	West Lancashire Light Railway (2ft gauge)
827	1903	0–4–0ST	Sybil	Conway Valley Museum (2ft gauge)
849	1904	0–4–0ST	Wild Aster	Llanberis Lake Railway (1ft 11½in gauge)
855	1904	0–4–0ST	Hugh Napier	Penrhyn Castle Museum (1ft 11½in gauge)
873	1905	0–4–0ST	Una	Brecon Mountain Railway (2ft gauge)
901	1906	2–6–2T	Russel	Welsh Highland Railway (2ft gauge)
920	1906	0–4–0ST	Pamela	J. Vernon, Newbold Verdon (1ft 10¾in gauge)
921	1906	0–4–0ST	Sybil Mary	J. Vernon Newbold Verdon (1ft 10¾in gauge)
994	1909	0–4–0ST	George Sholto	Bressingham (1ft 11½in gauge)
995	1909	0–4–0ST	Gertrude	Science Museum, Toronto, Canada
996	1909	0–4–0ST	Edward Sholto	Ontario, Canada (1ft 10¾in gauge)
1429	1922	0–4–0ST	No 1 Lady Joan	Knebworth Park (2ft gauge)
1430	922	0–4–0ST	Dolbadarn	Llanberis Lake Railway (1ft 11½in gauge)
1440	1923	0–6–0ST	Airedale	Yorkshire Dales Railway
1493	1925	0–4–0ST	No 11	Market Bosworth Light Railway
1589	1929	0–6–0ST	Newstead	M. Saul, Ware
1684	1931	0–4–0T		Somerset Railway Museum
1697	1932	0–6–0D	John Alcock	Middleton Railway
1709	1932	0–4–0ST	Michael	Ontario, Canada (1ft 10¾in gauge)
1800	1936	0–6–0ST	No 4 Robert Nelson	GCR/MLST
1842	1936	0–4–2ST	No 2 Lady Morrison	Hampshire Narrow Gauge Railway Society (2ft gauge)
1873	1937	0–6–0ST	Jessie	Norchard Steam Centre
1953	1939	0–6–0ST	Jacks Green	Nene Valley Railway
1954	1939	0–6–0ST	Kingley	Steamport Southport
1982	1940	0–6–0ST	Ring Haw	North Norfolk Railway
2280	1941	0–6–0ST		ISPS, Shanes Castle
2409	1941	0–6–0ST	King George	Titanic Steamship Co Ellastone

2411	1941	0–6–0ST	No 24	Corby & District Loco Society
2413	1941	0–6–0ST	*Gunby*	Chappel Steam Centre
2414	1941	0–6–0ST	*Spitfire*	Yorkshire Dales Railway
2765	1945	0–6–0SS	S119 *Beatrice*	Yorkshire Dales Railway
2855	1943	0–6–0ST	No 75006	Nene Valley Railway
2864	1943	0–6–0ST	No 48	Strathspey Railway
2879	1943	0–6–0ST		Brechin Railway Preservation Society
2890	1943	0–6–0ST	*Maureen*	Dart Valley Railway
3193	1943	0–6–0ST		Midland Railway Centre
3686	1948	0–6–0ST	No 60	Strathspey Railway
3698	1950	0–6–0ST	*Repulse*	L&HLR
3715	1952	0–6–0ST	*Primrose No 2*	Yorkshire Dales Railway
3777	1952	0–6–0ST	No 3777	North Staffordshire Railway
3781	1952	0–6–0ST	*Linda*	K&ESR
3782	1953	0–6–0ST		J. M. Walker, Oxford,
3783	1953	0–6–0ST	No 1	Yorkshire Dales Railway
3785	1953	0–6–0ST	No 69	Yorkshire Dales Railway
3790	1952	0–6–0ST	*Castle Hedingham*	Colne Valley Railway
3791	1952	0–6–0ST	*Holmon F. Stephens*	K&ESR
3792	1953	0–6–0ST	*Waggoner*	Marchwood WD Depot
3793	1953	0–6–0ST	*Shropshire*	Severn Valley Railway
3794	1953	0–6–0ST	*Cumbria*	L&HLR
3796	1953	0–6–0ST	*Errol Lonsdale*	Mid-Hants Railway
3797	1953	0–6–0ST	*Sapper*	K&ESR
3798	1953	0–6–0ST	No 98 *Royal Engineer*	Long Marsden, WD Depot
3800	1953	0–6–0ST	No 24 *William H. Austin*	K&ESR
3806	1953	0–6–0ST		Norchard Steam Centre
3810	1954	0–6–0ST	*Glendower*	Dart Valley Railway
3815	1954	2–6–2T	No 85	W&LLR (2ft 6in gauge)
3839	1956	0–6–0ST	*Wimblebury*	Foxfield Light Railway
3850	1958	0–6–0ST	*Juno*	Quainton Road
3890	1964	0–6–0ST	No 66	Quainton Road
4369	1951	0–4–0DM		Science Museum, Kensington (1ft 11½in gauge)

Kerr Stuart & Co Ltd, Stoke-on-Trent

720	1900	0–4–0WT	*Bonnie Dundee*	R&ER
721	1902	0–4–0WT	No 2	Narrow Gauge Museum, Tywyn (2ft 11in gauge)
886	1904	0–4–2ST	*Premier*	S&KLR (2ft 6in gauge)
926	1906	0–4–2ST	*Leader*	S&KLR (2ft 6in gauge)
1049	1908	0–4–2ST	*Excelsior*	Whipsnade Zoo (2ft 6in gauge)
1158	1917	0–4–0WT	*Diana*	Brecon Mountain Railway
2395	1917	0–4–2T		Bressingham (1ft 11½in gauge)
2405	1915	0–6–0T	No 1	West Lancashire Light Railway (600mm gauge)
2442	1915	0–6–0T		NGC Blaenau Ffestiniog
2451	1915	0–6–0T		NGC Blaenau Ffestiniog
3010	1916	0–6–0T		NGC Blaenau Ffestiniog
3014	1916	0–6–0T		NGC Blaenau Ffestiniog (2ft gauge)
3024	1916	0–4–2ST	No 1 *Lady Morrison*	Alan Keef, Oxford (3ft gauge)
3063	1918	0–4–0WT		Fairfields, Chepstow
3114	1918	0–4–0ST	*Ashover*	NGC Blaenau Ffestiniog
3117	1918	0–6–0T	*Sgt Murphy*	Cadeby Light Railway (2ft gauge)
4034	1920	0–6–2T	*Superior*	Whipsnade Zoo (2ft 6in gauge)
4047	1921	0–4–2ST	*Edward Thomas*	Talyllyn Railway (2ft 3in gauge)
4167	1920	0–4–0ST	*Moss Bay*	Shugborough Museum, Staffs

Works No.	Year	Wheel Argt.	Name	Location
4219	1924	0–4–2ST	Melior	S&KLR (2ft 6in gauge)
4250	1922	0–4–0ST	Lorna Doone	Birmingham Science Museum (2ft gauge)
4256	1922	0–4–0ST	Peter Pan	Available for hire (2ft gauge)
4260	1922	0–4–0ST	Pixie	LBLR (2ft gauge)
4404	1927	0–6–2ST	Joan	W&LLR (2ft 6in gauge)
4421	1929	0–6–0D		For Preservation
4428	1929	0–4–0D		Quainton Road
4449	1930	0–6–0PT	GWR 7714	Severn Valley Railway
4450	1930	0–6–0PT	GWR 7715	Quainton Road

Kitson & Co, Leeds

Works No.	Year	Wheel Argt.	Name	Location
T56	1882	0–4–0	Tram Engine	Hull Museum
T84	1883	0–4–0	Tram Engine	Belfast Museum
2509	1883	0–6–0PT		North of England Museum, Beamish
3799	1898	0–4–0ST		Somerset Railway Museum
4263	1904	0–6–2T	No 29	NYMR
5459	1933	0–6–0ST	Austin No 1	Llangollen Railway Society
5469	1933	0–6–0ST	No 44 Conway	South Cambridgeshire Museum
5470	1933	0–6–0ST	No 45 Colwyn	North Norfolk Railway
5474	1934	0–6–0ST	No 47 Carnarvon	Worcester Locomotive Society

Stephen Lewin, Dorset Foundery, Poole

Works No.	Year	Wheel Argt.	Name	Location
	1863	0–4–0ST		North of England Museum, Beamish

Manning Wardle & Co Ltd, Leeds

Works No.	Year	Wheel Argt.	Name	Location
641	1877	0–6–0ST	Solomon	Bressingham
865	1882	0–6–0ST	Aldwyth	Gwili Railway
1207	1890	0–6–0ST	The Welshman	Lound Hall Museum
1210	1890	0–6–0ST	Sir Berkeley	K&WVR
1317	1895	0–6–0ST	No 35	Foxfield Light Railway
1382	1897	0–4–0ST	Jubilee	Narrow Gauge Museum, Tywyn (1ft 11½in gauge)
1472	1900	0–4–0ST	Gervase	K&ESR
1532	1901	0–6–0ST		Heydon, Cambridgeshire
1601	1903	0–6–0ST	Arthur	K&ESR
1675	1906	0–6–0ST	No 8	Welland Valley Traction Club, Market Harborough
1762	1910	0–6–0ST	Dolobran	K&ESR
1795	1912	0–4–0ST	No 14	Northants Ironstone Railway Trust, Hunsbury Hill
1877	1915	0–6–2T	Chevalier	Whipsnade Zoo (2ft 6in gauge)
1955	1917	0–6–0ST	Charwelton	K&ESR
2009	1921	0–6–0ST	Rhyl	K&ESR
2010	1921	0–6–0ST	Rhondda	Caister Castle, Norfolk
2015	1921	0–6–0ST	Abernant	Aston Playground, Birmingham
2018	1922	0–6–0ST	Littleton No 5	GCR/MLST
2025	1923	0–6–0ST	Winston Churchill	Dudley Corporation, Black Country Museum
2047	1926	0–6–0ST	Warwickshire	Severn Valley Railway

Markham & Co Ltd, Chesterfield

Works No.	Year	Wheel Argt.	Name	Location
109	1894	0–4–0ST	Gladys	Midland Railway Centre

Metrovicks, Sheffield

	1912	0–4–0E		Chappel Steam Centre

Nasmyth, Wilson & Co Ltd, Patricroft

454	1894	0–4–2ST	No 4	Midland Railway Centre
828	1907	2–6–4T	No 4 *Meenglass*	Dr Ralph Cox, in store (3ft gauge)
829	1907	2–6–4T	No 5 *Drumbae*	Dr Ralph Cox, in store (3ft gauge)

Neilson & Co Ltd (later Neilson Reid & Co Ltd) Glasgow

1561	1870	0–4–0WT	No 1	Penrhyn Castle Museum
2203	1876	0–4–0ST	No 13 *Kelton Fell*	SRPS, Falkirk
2937	1882	0–4–0ST	No 11	Chasewater Light Railway
4004	1890	0–6–0CT	*Snipey*	Lytham Motive Power Museum
4444	1892	0–4–0T	No 1	Bressingham
5087	1896	0–4–0ST	No 25	Bressingham
5710	1902	0–6–0T	No 1 *Lord Roberts*	SRPS, Falkirk
5907	1901	0–4–0ST	No 9	Bass Museum, Burton-on-Trent

North British Locomotive Co Ltd, Glasgow

18386	1902	0–4–0ST	No 20	Lytham Motive Power Museum
24564	1939	0–6–0T	*Coventry No 1*	Quainton Road

Davey Paxman Ltd, Colchester

	1923	2–8–2	*River Esk*	R&ER
	1925	4–6–2	No 1 *Green Goddess*	Romney, Hythe and Dymchurch Railway (1ft 3 in gauge)
	1925	4–6–2	No 2 *Northern Chief*	RHDR
	1926	4–6–2	No 3 *Southern Maid*	RHDR
	1926	4–6–2	No 5 *Hercules*	RHDR
	1926	4–8–2	No 6 *Samson*	RHDR
	1926	4–6–2	No 7 *Typhoon*	RHDR
	1926	4–6–2	No 8 *Hurricane*	RHDR

Peckett & Sons, Bristol

614	1896	0–4–0ST	*Bear*	S&KLR
737	1899	0–4–0ST	*Daphne*	Skelmersdale New Town
783	1899	0–4–0T	*Lee Moor No 1*	Cornish China Clay Museum, St Austell (4ft 6in gauge)
784	1899	0–4–0T	*Lee Moor No 2*	Plymouth Railway Circle Museum, Plympton (4ft 6 in gauge)
830	1900	0–4–0ST		Lytham Motive Power Museum
917	1902	0–4–0ST		Chasewater Light Railway
933	1903	0–4–0ST	*Henry Cort*	Foxfield Light Railway
1008	1903	0–6–0ST	*Jurassic*	Lincolnshire Coast Railway (60cm gauge)
1026	1904	0–4–0T	No 1 *Tyrone*	Shanes Castle (3ft gauge)
1097	1906	0–4–0T	No 2	Belfast Museum (1ft 8in gauge)
1159	1908	0–4–0ST	*Annie*	East Lancashire Railway
1163	1908	0–4–0ST	*Whitehead*	West Somerset Railway
1257	1912	0–4–0ST	*Uppingham*	Market Overton
1270	1911	0–6–0ST	*Triassic*	Knebworth Park Railway (1ft 11½in gauge)
1316	1913	0–6–0ST	*Scaldwell*	Brockham Museum (3ft gauge)
1327	1913	0–6–0ST	*Mesozoic*	Brecon Mountain Railway (2ft gauge)
1351	1914	0–4–0ST	*The Colonel*	Chasewater Light Railway
1370	1915	0–4–0ST	*May*	Steamtown, Carnforth
1376	1915	0–4–0ST	No 1	Lochty Railway

Works No.	Year	Wheel Argt.	Name	Location
1378	1914	0–6–0ST	Westminster	K&ESR
1393	1915	0–4–0ST		Victoria Ironworks, Dalaston
1430	1916	0–4–0ST	Adam	Cambrian Railways Society
1438	1916	0–4–0ST		Titanic Steamship Co, Ellastone
1547	1919	0–4–0ST	Victory	Midland Railway Centre
1555	1920	0–4–0ST		Riber Castle Wildlife Park, Matlock
1567	1920	0–6–0ST	Acton Hall No 3	Llangollen Railway Society
1579	1921	0–4–0ST	Pectin	Bulmer Railway Centre
1611	1923	0–4–0ST		
1631	1923	0–4–0T		K&ESR
1632	1923	0–6–0ST	Liassic	In Canada (1ft 11½in gauge)
1636	1924	0–4–0ST	Fonmon	Bristol Industrial Railway
1690	1926	0–4–0ST	No 1690	Dart Valley Railway
1722	1926	0–4–0ST	Rocket	Birmingham Railway Museum, Tyseley
1738	1928	0–4–0ST	No 4	Severn Valley Railway
1756	1928	0–4–0ST	Hornpipe	Quainton Road
1759	1928	0–4–0ST	Elizabeth	Market Overton
1788	1929	0–6–0ST	Kilmersdon	West Somerset Railway
1870	1934	0–6–0ST	Banshee	Northants Ironstone Trust
1871	1934	0–6–0ST	No 86	Northants Ironstone Trust
1893	1936	0–4–0ST	No 2	Titanic Steamship Co, Ellastone
1900	1936	0–4–0T	Jill	Quainton Road
1903	1936	0–4–0ST	No 1903	Gwili Railway
1925	1937	0–4–0ST	No 1 Caliban	L&HLR
1940	1937	0–4–0ST	Henbury	Bristol Industrial Museum
1963	1938	0–4–0ST	Hilda	GCR/MLST
1967	1939	0–4–0ST	Merlin/Myrddin	Gwili Railway
1970	1939	0–6–0ST	No 5 John D. Hammer	North Norfolk Railway
1976	1939	0–4–0ST		Titanic Steamship Co, Ellastone
1999	1941	0–4–0T	North Western Gas Board	Steamport, Southport
2000	1941	0–6–0ST		Nene Valley Railway
2003	1941	0–4–0ST	No 2003	Middleton Railway
2004	1941	0–4–0ST	No 1	Birmingham Railway Museum, Tyseley
2012	1941	0–4–0ST	Herbert	Market Bosworth Light Railway
2024	1942	0–4–2ST		Welsh Highland Railway (2ft gauge)
2029	1942	0–6–0ST	No 87	Northants Ironstone Trust
2031	1942	0–4–0ST		Dart Valley Railway
2039	1943	0–4–0ST		Chappel Steam Centre
2050	1944	0–6–0ST	No 1	Ffestiniog Railway (1ft 11½in gauge)
2081	1947	0–4–0ST	Volunteer	Foxfield Light Railway
2085	1948	0–4–0ST	Foleshill	Yorkshire Dales Railway
2087	1948	0–4–0ST	Miranda	Steamtown, Carnforth
2088	1948	0–4–0ST		Birmingham Railway Museum, Tyseley
2104	1950	0–4–0ST		Quainton Road
2105	1951	0–4–0ST		Quainton Road
2110	1950	0–4–0ST		Market Overton
2111	1949	0–4–0ST	Blackpool	Lytham Motive Power Museum
2129	1952	0–4–0ST	James	Quainton Road
2130	1952	0–4–0ST	No 7	Market Bosworth Light Railway

2131	1951	0–4–0ST	No 6	Cambrian Railways Society
2147	1952	0–4–0ST	*Uskmouth No 1*	Norchard Steam Centre
2150	1954	0–6–0ST	*Mardy No 1*	Swanage Railway
2153	1954	0–4–0ST	No 5	Steamport, Southport
2154	1954	0–4–0F		Irlam Recreation Ground

Sentinel Steam Waggon & Carriage Co Ltd, Shrewsbury

6155	1925	0–4–0VBT		Ironbridge Gorge Museum
6158	1925	0–4–0VBT		Ironbridge Gorge Museum
6515	1926	4WVBTG	*Isebrooke*	Quainton Road
6807	1928	0–4–0TG	No 10 *Gervase*	K&ESR
7109	1927	4WVBTG	*Joyce*	W. H. McAlpine, Fawley
7232	1927	4WVBTG	*Ann*	Yorkshire Dales Railway
7492	1928	4WVBTG	*Fry*	G. R. Finbow, Bacton, Suffolk
7701	1929	4WVBTG	*Nutty*	Narrow Gauge Museum, Tywyn (2ft 6in gauge)
8024	1929	4WVBTG	*Gasbag*	Steamtown, Carnforth
8837	1933	4WVBTG	LNER No 54	Middleton Railway
9365	1945	4WVBTG		Northamptonshire Ironstone Railway Trust
9366	1945	4WVBTG	No 11	Quainton Road
9369	1946	4WVBTG		Northamptonshire Ironstone Railway Trust
9370	1947	4WVBTG	No 1	Midland Railway Centre
9373	1947	4WVBTG	*St Monans*	GCR/MLST
9374	1947	4WVBTG		Children's Playground, Frome
9376	1947	4WVBTG	No 7	Quainton Road
9387	1948	4WVBTG		Welshmill Adventure Playground, Frome
9355	1952	4WVBTG		Foxfield Railway
9537	1952	4WVBTG	*Susan*	Lytham Motive Power Museum
9559	1954	4WVBTG		Tanfield Railway
9596	1955	4WVBTG		Llangollen Railway Society
9622	1958	4WVBTG	*Swansea Vale No 1*	Brecon Mountain Railway
9629	1957	4WVBTG	No 5	NYMR
9632	1957	4WVBTG	*Teeside No 5*	Midland Railway Centre

Sharp Stewart & Co Ltd

1435	1863	0–4–0ST	FR No 18	Hartwell Trading Centre, Barrow
1585	1865	0–4–0ST	FR No 25	Stonecross School, Ulverston
	1895	0–4–4T	*Dunrobin*	Fort Steele Museum, British Columbia
4150	1896	4–8–0		Whipsnade Zoo (3ft 6in gauge)

W. Spence, Cork Street Foundry, Dublin, Ireland

	1895	0–4–0T	No 13	Narrow Gauge Museum, Tywyn (1ft 10in gauge)
	1895	0–4–0T	No 15	ISPS, Shane's Castle (1ft 10in gauge)
	1902	0–4–0T	No 17	Guinness Brewery, Ireland (1ft 10in gauge)
	1905	0–4–0T	No 20	Belfast Transport Museum (1ft 10in gauge)
	1905	0–4–0T	No 20	Winn Technology, County Cork (1ft 10in gauge)
	1921	0–4–0T	No 23	Brockham Museum Trust (1ft 10in gauge)

Works No.	Year	Wheel Argt.	Name	Location
Robert Stephenson & Co Ltd, Newcastle on Tyne				
2309	1879	0–6–0T	*Haydock*	Penrhyn Castle Museum
2613	1884	4–4–0T	No 2	Belfast Museum
2614	1884	4–4–0T	No 3	Steamtown Museum, Vermont, USA
2730	1891	0–6–0T	*Twizell*	North of England Museum, Beamish
2854	1898	2–4–0CT	No E1	North of England Museum, Beamish
3377	1909	0–6–2T	No 5	NYMR
Robert Stephenson & Hawthorn Ltd, Darlington & Newcastle on Tyne				
6947	1938	0–6–0ST	No 39	GCR/MLST
7006	1940	0–4–0CT	*Roker*	Foxfield Light Railway
7007	1940	0–4–0CT	*Hendon*	Tanfield Railway
7031	1941	0–6–0ST	No 54	Chappel Steam Centre
7035	1940	0–6–0ST	No 62	Ashby Playing Fields
7058	1942	0–4–0ST	No 7058	Gwili Railway
7063	1943	0–6–0ST	*Eustace Forth*	North Yorkshire Moors Railway
7069	1942	0–4–0CT	*Southwick*	Dinting Railway Centre
7070	1942	0–4–0CT	*Millfield*	Bressingham
7086	1943	0–6–0ST		K&ESR
7097	1943	0–6–0ST	No 9 *Cairngorm*	Strathspey Railway
7098	1942	0–6–0ST	No 9	Tanfield Railway
7136	1944	0–6–0ST	*Warrington*	Dinting Railway Centre
7169	1944	0–6–0ST	No 68005	East Somerset Railway
7214	1945	0–4–0ST	*George*	RSH Ltd. Spondon
7289	1944	0–6–0ST	*Fred*	K&WVR
7409	1948	0–4–0ST	*Sir Cecil A. Cochrane*	Tanfield Railway
7493	1948	0–4–0ST	*Mars 11*	Leicester Museum
7537	1949	0–6–0T	No 3	Market Bosworth Light Railway
7544	1949	0–4–0ST	*Bonnie Prince Charlie*	Didcot Railway Centre
7597	1949	0–6–0T		Chappel Steam Centre
7609	1950	0–6–0T	No 31 *Meteor*	NYMR
7661	1950	0–4–0ST	No 2	Yorkshire Dales Railway
7667	1950	0–6–0ST	No 26	K&ESR
7668	1950	0–6–0ST	No 57	K&WVR
7671	1950	0–6–0ST	*Jupiter*	Chappel Steam Centre
7673	1950	0–6–0ST	No 62	K&WVR
7683	1951	0–6–0T	MEA No 2	Bury Transport Museum
7684	1951	0–6–0T	No 4	Market Bosworth Light Railway
7705	1950	0–4–0ST		Caerphilly Railway Society
7745	1952	0–6–0T	No 2	Boyne Falls, USA
7760	1953	0–6–0ST	No 44	Tanfield Railway
7761	1950	0–6–0ST	No 63	K&WVR
7763	1954	0–6–0T	No 38	Tanfield Railway
7765	1954	0–6–0T	No 40	Colne Valley Railway
7796	1954	0–4–0ST	No 21	Tanfield Railway
7800	1954	0–6–0ST	No 47	Didcot Railway Centre
7803	1954	0–4–0F		Bressingham
7845	1955	0–6–0T	No 12	North Norfolk Railway
7846	1955	0–6–0T		Chappel Steam Centre
7849	1955	0–6–0ST	No 47 *Moorbarrow*	NYMR
7944	1957	0–6–0ST	No 16	Tanfield Railway

Vulcan Foundry

1828	1902	0–4–0ST	*Vulcan*	Lytham Motive Power Museum
5200	1945	2–8–0	WD 79257	K&WVR
5309	1945	0–6–0ST	No 12	Colne Valley Railway

De Winton & Co, Caernarvon & Alexander Chaplin & Co, Glasgow

	1877	0–4–0VBT	*Kathaleen*	NGC Blaenau Ffestiniog (1ft 10¾in gauge)
	1877	0–4–0T	*George Henry*	Narrow Gauge Museum, Tywyn (1ft 11½in gauge)
	1877	0–4–0VBT	No 1 *Chaloner*	LBLR (2ft gauge)
	1893	0–4–0VBT	*Watkin*	Penrhyn Castle Museum (3ft gauge)
	1894	0–4–0VBT	*Pendyffryn*	Brecon Mountain Railway (2ft gauge)
	1895	0–4–0VBT	*Llanfair*	NGC Blaenau Ffestiniog (3ft gauge)

Yorkshire Engine Co Ltd, Sheffield

2229	1927	2–8–2	No 8 *River Esk*	Ravenglass & Eskdale Railway
2294	1931	4–6–2	No 10 *Doctor Syn*	RHDR
2295	1931	4–6–2	No 9 *Winston Churchill*	RHDR
2474	1949	0–4–0ST	*City Link*	Yorkshire Dales Railway
2498	1951	0–6–0ST	*Chislet*	Quainton Road
2521	1952	0–6–0ST	No 9	Lound Hall Museum, Mansfield

Index of Foreign Built Locomotives

This table is complete as far as is possible to 1978, but the import of locomotives from abroad shows signs of continuing to some extent.

American Locomotive Co, Schenectady, USA, (ALCO)

57165	1916	2–6–2T	*Mountaineer*	Festiniog Railway (1ft 11½in gauge)

Baldwin Locomotive Works, Philadelphia, USA

29587	1902		Electric Loco	Royal Scottish Museum, Edinburgh
49604	1918	2–4–0DM	No 11 *Moelwyn*	Festiniog Railway (1ft 11½in gauge)
61269	1930	4–6–2	N2	Brecon Mountain Rly, Pontsticill (2ft gauge)

A. Borsig, Berlin, Germany

6022	1906	0–6–2T	No 7 *Sotillos*	In store (60cm gauge)

Corpet Louvet et Cie, Seine, France

493	1888	0–6–0T	*Cambrai*	Alan Keef Ltd

Couillet Marcinelle, Belgium

1140	1895	0–6–0T	No 1 *Sabero*	In store (60cm gauge)
1209	1898	0–6–0T	No 2 *Sahelices*	In store (60cm gauge)
1318	1900	0–6–0T	No 3 *Olleros*	In store (60cm gauge)

Franco Belge, Raismes, France

2855	1944	0–8–0T	*Sir Drefaldwyn*	W&LLR (2ft 6in gauge)

Works No.	Year	Wheel Argt.	Name	Location
Fricks of Aarhus, Denmark				
89	1928	2–6–4T	No 740	Nene Valley Railway
360	1949	0–6–0T	No 656	Nene Valley Railway
General Electric, Erie, USA				
30483	1949	0–4–4–0DE	*Esso*	Steamtown, Carnforth
Hartman, Denmark				
2110	1895	0–4–0WT		Middleton Railway
Henschel & Son, Kassel, Germany				
10745	1911	4–6–0	No 3.628	Nene Valley Railway
28035	1948	0–4–0T	No 5 *Helen Kathryn*	Llanberis Lake Railway (1ft 11½in gauge)
16043	1918	0–4–0T	No 102	In store (60cm gauge)
16045	1918	0–4–0T	No 103	In store (60cm gauge)
16073	1918	0–4–2T	No 101	In store (60cm gauge)
Jung, Germany				
939	1906	0–4–0WT	*Justine*	Dowty RPS (1ft 11½in gauge)
1261	1908	0–6–2WT	No 99-3553	Brecon Mountain Railway (2ft gauge)
3872	1931	0–6–0T	No 14	Alan Keef, Oxford (2ft gauge)
7509	1937	0–4–0WT	*Ginette Marie*	Llanberis Lake Railway (1ft 11½in gauge)
Kraus, Munich				
8738	1926	0–4–0TT	*The Bug*	RHDR
Krupp of Essen				
1662	1937	4–6–2	*Mannertreu*	Bressingham (1ft 3in gauge)
1663	1937	4–6–2T	*Rosenkavalier*	Bressingham (1ft 3in gauge)
1664	1937	4–6–2	No 11 *Black Prince*	RHDR (1ft 3in gauge)
11535	1935	2–6–2T	No 064-305	Nene Valley Railway
Lima Locomotive Co, Ohio, USA				
8758	1945	2–8–0	PSR N0 203-474	K&WVR
8939	1945	2–8–2	SNCF 1–4–1R No 73	Bressingham
Motala, Sweden				
516	1914	2–6–2T	No 1178	Nene Valley Railway
Nydqvist Och Holm, Norway				
1163	1919	2–6–0	NSR N0 376	K&ESR
1164	1919	2–6–0	*King Haakon 7*	GCR/MLST
2082	1944	4–6–0	No 1697	Nene Valley Railway
2229	1953	2–6–4T	No 1928	Nene Valley Railway
Orenstein & Koppel, Berlin, Germany				
73	1900	0–4–0WT	*Penlee*	Newlyn, Cornwall (2ft gauge)
5668	1912	0–4–0WT	*Eigiau*	Bressingham (1ft 11½in gauge)
5834	1912	0–4–0WT	*P. C. Allen*	LBLR (2ft gauge)
7529	1914	0–4–0WT		Cadeby Light Railway (2ft gauge)
10808	1924	0–6–0WT	*Pedemoura*	Welsh Highland Railway (2ft gauge)
12722	1936	0–4–0WT	No 9	Brecon Mountain Railway (60cm gauge)

11784	1925	0–6–0WT	*Sao Domingos*	Knebworth Park Railway (2ft gauge)
12740	1936	0–6–0T	No 5 *Elf*	LBLR (2ft gauge)

Paris Lyons & Mediterranean Railway (PLM)

	1936	4–6–2	No 231K22	Steamtown, Carnforth

Sabero

	1937	0–6–0T	No 6 *La Herrera*	In store (60cm gauge)

Schickau Elbing, Germany

5865	1944	2–10–0		Bressingham

Scwarzkopf, Berlin

9124	1927	0–4–0WT	*Bronhilde*	Bressingham (1ft 11½in gauge)
10808	1924	0–6–0WT	*Pedemoura*	Welsh Highland Railway
01.1104	1940	4–6–2		Steamtown, Carnforth

Tubize, Finland

2369	1948	2–6–2T		M. Knight, Biddenden (2ft 6in gauge)

Vulcan Ironworks, USA

4432	1943	0–6–0T	No 30064	Bluebell Railway
4433	1943	0–6–0T	No 21 *Wainwright*	K&ESR
4441	1943	0–6–0T	No 22 *Maunsell*	K&ESR
4446	1943	0–6–0T	No 72	K&WVR

Vulcan-Wenke

12518	1934	0–8–0	No 99.3461	Knebworth Park Railway (2ft gauge)

Wolf, Germany

1228	1927	0–6–0T		Steamtown, Carnforth

Principal Centres of Preserved Locomotives

Principal Museums With Static Locomotives

Darlington, North Road Station; Great Western Museum, Swindon; National Railway Museum, York.

Other Museums

Belfast Transport Museum; Birmingham Museum of Science and Industry; Bristol City Museum; Caerphilly Railway Society, Former TVR Works, Caerphilly (not open to the public); China Clay Museum, St Austell, Cornwall; City of Liverpool Museum; Coalbrookdale Works Museum; Conway Valley Museum; Hull Transport Museum; Industrial Railway Museum, Penrhyn Castle, Bangor, Caernarvon; London Transport Museum, Covent Garden; Museum of Science & Engineering, Newcastle-upon-Tyne; Museum of Transport, Glasgow; Narrow Gauge Railway Centre, Gloddfa Ganol, Blaenau Festiniog, North Wales; National Coal Board Mining Museum, Loundhill, Mansfield, Notts; North West of Ireland Railway Society, Shanes Castle; Port Erin Museum, Isle of Man; Royal Scottish Museum, Edinburgh; Science Museum, Kensington, London; Shugborough Hall, Staffordshire; County Industrial Museum, Great Haywood; Somerset Railway Museum, Bleadon and Uphill, Somerset; Swansea Industrial and Maritime Museum; Telford (Horsehay) Steam Trust and Ironbridge Gorge Museum, Telford, Shropshire; Titanic Steamship Co, Ellastone, Staffs (not open to the public); Tyne and Wear County Council, Monkwearmouth Station Museum; Tywyn Narrow Gauge Railway Museum, Tywyn (Headquarters of Talyllyn Railway).

Fully Operational Lines

Lines of a mile or more up to several miles over which trains are worked to published time-tables. They are usually operational only during weekends during the summer months, but some also run midweek services, and in a few cases, such as Keighley & Worth Valley, where a limited service is run all the year round.

Bluebell Railway, Horsted Keynes, Sussex; Chasewater Light Railway Preservation Society, Brownhills, Staffs; Dart Valley Railway, Buckfastleigh, Devon; Dart Valley Railway (Torbay Line); East Somerset Railway, Cranmore, Somerset; Foxfield Light Railway, Blyth Bridge, Stoke-on-Trent; GCR Main Line Steam Trust, Loughborough, Leicestershire; Gwili Railway, Carmarthen; Isle of Wight Steam Railway, Haven Street, Isle of Wight; Keighley & Worth Valley Railway, Haworth, Yorkshire; Kent & East Sussex Railway, Tenterden, Kent; Lakeside & Haverthwaite Railway, Lancashire; Lochty Railway, Fife; Market Bosworth Light Railway, Leicestershire; Middleton Railway, Leeds; Mid-Hants Railway, Alresford, Hampshire; Nene Valley Railway, Peterborough, Northants; North Yorkshire Moors Railway, Grosmont, Yorkshire; Severn Valley Railway, Bridgnorth, Shropshire; Strathspey Railway, Aviemore, Scotland; West Somerset Railway, Minehead, Somerset.

Museums and Steam Centres

Centres at which engines are steamed at various times, with lengths of track varying from a few hundred yards or so up to a mile, over which they can run, either with a coach for the benefit of visitors, or in some cases giving footplate rides. In some cases there are plans to obtain longer stretches of lines with a view to running fully operational train services).

Bowes Railway, Durham; Bressingham Hall, Diss, Norfolk; Bristol Industrial Museum, Princes Wharf, Bristol; Brockham Museum, near Dorking, Surrey (narrow gauge); Bulmer's Railway Centre, Hereford; Caerphilly Railway Society, former Taff Vale Works (not normally open to the public); Colne Valley Railway, Castle Hedingham; Norchard Steam Centre, Norchard, near Lydney, Glos; Dinting Railway Centre, Glossop, Derbyshire; Dowty Railway Preservation Society, Ashchurch, Glos; East Lancashire Railway Preservation Society, Bury, Lancs; Great Western Society, Didcot Railway Centre, Oxfordshire; Lytham Motive Power Museum, Lytham, Lancs; Midland Railway Trust, Butterley near Ripley, Derbyshire; Morris, R. P., Longfield, Kent (narrow gauge);

North of England Open Air Museum, Beamish, Durham; Quainton Railway Society, Quainton Road Station, near Aylesbury, Bucks; Railway Preservation Society of Ireland, Whitehead, Belfast; Scottish Railway Preservation Society, Falkirk; Standard Gauge Steam Trust, Tyseley, Birmingham; Steamport, Southport, Lancs; Steamtown, Carnforth, Lancs; Chappel Steam Centre, Chappel & Wakes Colne, Essex; Tanfield Railway, Marley Hill, Durham; Yorkshire Dales Railway, Embsay, Yorkshire.

Other Projects

Projects not yet operational, 1979, and in some cases only in the planning stage.

Brecon Mountain Railway, Pontsticill (narrow gauge) – Hills & Bailey; Bristol Suburban Railway, Bitton, Bristol – Mangotsfield – Bath; Cambrian Railways Society, Oswestry; Llangollen Railway Society; North Stafford Railway Society, Cheddleton; Peak Railway Society, Matlock – Buxton; Swanage Railway Company Ltd.

Section 5

Narrow Gauge full length lines of several miles

Festiniog Railway; Isle of Man Steam Railway; Ravenglass & Eskdale Railway; Romney, Hythe & Dymchurch Railway; Talyllyn Railway; Welshpool & Llanfair Railway.

Section 6

Other shorter narrow gauge lines

Bicton Woodland Railway, Budleigh Salterton, Devon; Bala Lake Railway, Merioneth, Wales; Cadeby Light Railway, Hinckley, Leics; Hampshire Light Railway and Museum, Durley, Hants; Hollycombe Woodland Railway, Liphook, Hants; Knebworth Park, Stevenage, Herts; Leighton Buzzard Light Railway; Lincolnshire Coast Light Railway, Humberstone, Grimsby; Llanberis Lake Railway; Shanes Castle Sittingbourne & Kemsley Light Railway; West Lancashire Light Railway, Hesketh Bank, Preston, Lancs; Whipsnade Zoo; The Vale of Rheidol Railway, Aberystwyth, still worked by British Railways; its only steam line, and Snowdon Mountain Railway are not included, as these are still run on a strictly commercial basis, and do not come within the category of preserved lines.

In addition there are also numerous miniature lines with a gauge of 15in or less to be found throughout the country, usually at pleasure resorts and which operate only during the holiday months.

Photo Credits

Anderson, D. A.   55(B)
Ashby, R.   75(T)
Ashworth, B. J.   13(B)

Ballard, B.   159(B)
Beamish, North of England Open Air
   Museum   129(B)
Bell, J. E.   69(B)
Bennett, K.   143(B)
Besley, J. R.   72(C)
Bide, K.   162(B)
Bird, J. H.   82(T)
Billington, M. H.   153(T)
Birch, D.   89(B)
Bloom, A.   168(B)
Boocock, C. P.   54(C), 82(B), 156(B), 169(C)
Boyes, J. M.   158
British Railways   9(T), 12(B), 35(B), 45(B), 49(B),
   63(B), 80(B), 108(B), 113(B), 126(T), 126(B)
Buckley, R. J.   119(B), 123(T), 147(B), 154(B), 160(B),
   163(B)
Burns, M.   115(T)

Canning, D. E.   128(C)
Carr, I. S.   16(B), 40(T), 91(B), 167(C)
Carter, J. R.   65(B)
Casserley, H. C.   9(B), 17(T), 35(T), 37, 62(T), 74(B),
   120(T), 121(T), 121(B), 131(B), 133(B), 139(B),
   142(B), 151(B), 156(T)
Casserley, R. M.   57(B), 130(T), 138(T), 138(B),
   143(T)
Coffin, R. O.   98(T)
Coombe, A. G.   87(B)
Cooper, G. P.   98(C)
Crompton, A. B.   162(T)
Crowder, I   78(B)
Cross, D. M.   105(T), 167(T)

Dauwalder, R.   92(T)
Davies, W. J. K.   32(B), 148(T)
Dyson, D. H.   101(T)

Eatwell, D.   36(T)
Edgington, T. J.   26(T), 56(T), 105(B), 141(T)
Evans, R. K.   30(T)

Fenn, S. A.   100(B)
Fitzgerald, J. D.   86(T)
Flinders, G. T.   87(T)
Flitcroft, D. A.   117(T)
Fozard, J.   93(B)
Friel, C. P.   21(B), 22(T), 59(T), 83(B), 96(T), 112(B),
   150(T)

Gater, L. P.   24(T)
Gomm, T. R.   17(B)
Goss, J.   116(T)
Gott, M.   169(B)
Great Western Society   54(B), 72(T)
Greenwood, D.   149, 153(B)
Greenwood, R. S.   44(T), 148(B)
Groom, P. H.   32(T), 106(B), 135(B), 152, 168(T)

Hall, M.   29(B), 38(T), 54(T), 55(T), 63(T), 123(B),
   125(T)
Harris, P.   88(B)
Harvey, J.   107(B)
Haydon, J. C.   42(T), 48(T)
Herbert, C. C. B.   64(T)
Heys, R.   51(T)
Higgins, R.   169(T)

Hodge, J.   61(B)
Holt, I. G.   41(B), 79(T), 142(T), 160(T)
Hood, J. S.   111(B)
Hooper, R.   85(C)
Hounsell, G. R.   50(T), 84, 89(T), 103, 104(B), 111(T),
   155
Hull Locomotive Preservation Group   99
Hunt, N. A.   22(B), 98(B), 134(B), 161(B)

Ian Allan Library   8, 11(T), 19(T), 24(B), 25, 28(B),
   34(B), 39(B), 40(B), 46(B), 52(T), 58(T), 61(T), 70,
   71(T), 74(T), 77(B), 78(B), 80(T), 85(T), 116(B),
   119(T), 120(B), 127(B)
Idle, D. A.   38(B), 60(T), 93(T), 95(T), 144
Illineworth, N.   102(B)
Imbush, J.   72(B)

Jaggers, K. A.   16(T)
John Adams Publicity Ltd   20(T)
Jones, F.   130(B), 137(B), 140(B)

K&WVRPS   47(B)
KJB Films   81(B)
King, D. K.   145(T)
King, G. D.   77(T), 141(B), 150(B), 163(T), 165
Knight, N. R.   41(T)

Lawrence, K. P.   113(T)
Lewis, R. E.   33
Locomotive Publishing Co   7(T), 10(T), 11(B), 13(T),
   15(T), 51(B), 59(B), 68(T), 69(T), 82(C), 83(T), 88(T)
London Transport Executive   18, 46(T)
Loudwell, B.   49(T)
Lowe, D. J.   92(C)
Luscombe, D.   50(B)

McIntyre, A. D.   128(B)
Main Line Steam Trust   167(C)
Massingham, C.   125(B)
Marshall, J.   44(B)
Marshall, L. G.   90(T)
Maxwell, S.   48(B)
Middleton Railway Association   43
Momson, G. W.   109(B)
Monk, R.   132(T)
Morrison, B.   47(T), 60(B), 85(B), 86(B), 115(B),
   135(T), 157(B)
Muggleton, D. E.   117(B)

National Railway Museum, Crown
   Copyright   10(B), 14, 20(B), 34(T)
Nicolle, B. J.   124(B)
Nicolson, L.   57(T), 114(T)
Nixon, L. A.   108(T), 118(B)

Oldham, E.   23(T)

Panting, R. A.   19(B), 56(B), 79(B)
Parkes, A. D.   95(B)
Patterson, E. M.   36(B)
Percival, D. L.   28(T), 64(B)
Peters, I.   21(T), 65(T)
Pirt, K. R.   76(T)
Preedy, N. E.   67(T), 92(B), 96(B), 100(T), 110(B),
   124(T)
Price, J. H.   39(T)

Real Photographs Co Ltd   107(T)
Relf, P. J.   45(T)
Riley, R. C.   29(T)
Ruffell, R. E.   101(B), 146(T)
Russell, R.   109(T)

St Leger, W. 15(B)
Sagar, J 73(T)
Science Museum 7(B)
Scottish Railway Preservation Society 42(B), 53(B), 139(T)
Scott-Lowe, G. 134(T)
Scrace, J. 31, 52(B), 62(B), 94, 97(B), 112(T), 122(T)
Sharpe, P. J. 12(T), 53(T), 91(T), 136, 161(T)
Siviter, R. E. B. 104(T)
Skelton, P. J. C. 127(T)
Smith, I. 129(T)
Stieber, R. 133(T)
Stephenson, B. 76(B)
Stephenson, T. 73(T)
Stevenson, R. A. 110(T)
Swain, A. 106(B)

Talyllyn Railway 166(T)
Tallet, R. 26(B)

Taylor, A. R. 90(B)
Titlow, J. 4, 75(T), 81(T)
Trevor-Rowe, D. 132(C), 132(B)
Tuffs, C. J. 92(T), 146(B)
Turner, C. L. 27
Turner, D. 66
Turvey, M. P. 68(B)

Vaughan, J. A. M. 128(T), 154(T), 157(T)

Wade, B. 122(B), 159(T)
Walker, C. P. 102(T)
Ward, P. 140(T)
Warman, I. M. 118(T)
Webb, B. 131(T)
Wheeler, G. 58(B)
Wildish, G. 151(T)
Wildsmith, R. 23(B), 30(B), 114(B)

Index

Index of Main and Passenger lines' locomotives, listed under railway of origin. This table does not include industrial or other privately owned locomotives which are listed separately elsewhere, as are foreign locomotives.

Alexandra Docks
0–4–0ST *Trojan* 54

Belfast & County Down
4–4–2T 62

Belfast & Northern Counties
Tram engines 35

British Railways
4–6–2 'Britannia' class 117
4–6–2 *Duke of Gloucester* 120
4–6–0 Class 5MT 73000 118
4–6–0 Class 5MT (Caprotti) 122
4–6–0 Class 5MT 75000 118
2–6–0 Class 4MT 76000 120
2–6–0 Class 2MT 78000 121
2–6–4T Class 4MT 80000 119
2–10–0 Class 9F 92000 127
Diesel Class 02 126
Diesel Class 03 124
Diesel Class 04 119
Diesel Class 07 128
Diesel Class 11 116
Diesel Class 24 125
Diesel Class 31 123
Diesel Class 35 'Hymek' 127
Diesel Class 42 'Warship' 125
Diesel Class 52 'Western' 128
Electric Class 71 126
Electric Class 76 117
Electric Class 84 127
Diesel 0–6–0DM 122
Diesel *Vulcan* 122
Diesel *Deltic* 121

Bury Port & Gwendraeth Valley
0–6–0ST 59

Caledonian
4–2–2 No 123 39
0–4–4T No 419 53
0–6–0 No 828 58

Canterbury & Whitstable
0–4–0 *Invicta* 11

Cardiff
0–4–0ST 55

Cavan & Leitrim
4–4–0T 36

City & South London
Electric 46

Corris
0–4–0ST No 3 31
0–4–0ST No 4 82

County Donegal
2–6–4T *Blanche* 74
Diesel *Phoenix* 95

Dublin & South Eastern
2–6–0 83

Duke of Sutherland
0–4–4T *Dunrobin* 51

Festiniog Railway
0–4–0ST 17
0–4–4–0T Fairlie 31

Furness
0–4–0 *Coppernob* 14
0–4–0ST 17

Glasgow & South Western
0–6–0T No 9 77

Great Central
2–8–0 Class O1 72
4–4–0 *Butler Henderson* 81

Great Eastern
2–4–0 No 490 46
4–6–0 No 61572 73
0–6–0 Class J15 36
0–6–0 Class J17 60
0–6–0T No 87 45
0–6–2T No 999 77
0–4–0ST No 229 31

Great Northern
4–2–2 No 1 23
4–4–2 No 990 55
4–4–2 No 251 64
0–6–2T No 4744 80
0–6–0ST No 1247 54

Great Northern (Ireland)
4–4–0 No 131   59
4–4–0 No 171   75
4–4–0 No 85 (Compound)   95
2–4–2T No 93   51

Great North of Scotland
4–4–0 Gordon Highlander   80

Great Southern & Western
2–2–2 No 36   15
0–6–0T No 90   30
0–6–0 Class J15 No 184   21
0–6–0 Class J15 No 186   21

Great Southern
4–6–0 No 800 Maeve   106

Great Western
2–2–2 North Star (replica)   12
0–4–0T Tiny   22
4–4–0 City of Truro   61
4–6–0 Lode Star   68
4–6–0 'Castle' class   84
4–6–0 'King' class   89
4–6–0 'Hall' class   92
4–6–0 'Manor' class   105
4–4–0 'Dukedog' class   104
0–4–2T 14xx class   96
2–6–2 45xx class   68
2–6–2T 5101 class   66
2–6–2T 61xx class   66
0–6–2T 56xx class   87
0–6–0PT 57xx class   93
0–6–0PT 64xx class   96
0–6–0PT 16xx class   115
0–6–0PT 94xx class   113
0–6–0PT 1366 class   101
0–6–0ST 1361 class   72
0–6–0PT 15xx class   114
0–6–0 'Dean Goods' No 2516   35
0–6–0 2251 class   95
2–8–0 28xx class   65
2–6–0 43xx class   74
2–8–2T 72xx class   98
2–8–0 42xx class   72

Groudle Glen
2–4–0T   57

Gwendraeth Valley
0–6–0ST Margaret   32

Highland
4–6–0 No 103   50

Isle of Man
2–4–0T   26
0–6–0T   38

Kent & East Sussex
0–6–0T No 3 Bodiam   24

Lancashire & Yorkshire
2–4–2T No 1008   44
0–6–0 Barton Wright   30
0–6–0ST Barton Wright   47
0–6–0 Aspinall   43
0–4–0ST   47
0–4–0ST Wren   41
0–4–0 Petrol tractor   80

Liverpool & Manchester
Rocket   10
Lion   12

London & North Western
2–2–2 Columbine   13
2–2–2 Cornwall   14
2–4–0 Hardwick   26
0–6–2T No 1054   33
0–8–0 No 49395   82
0–4–0ST No 1439   19
0–4–0ST Pet   20

London & South Western
2–4–0T Beattie   27
4–4–2T Adams   34
4–4–0 Adams No 563   49
4–4–0 Drummond No 120   58
4–6–0 Urie S15 class   82
0–4–4T Drummond M7 class   53
0–4–4T Adams O2 class   45
0–4–0T Adams B4 class   48

London, Brighton & South Coast
Electric No DS75   56
0–6–0T 'Terriers'   24
0–6–0T E1 class   29
0–4–2 Gladstone   33
0–6–2T Birch Grove   56

London, Midland & Scottish
0–6–0 4F class   85
0–6–0T 'Jinty'   86
2–8–0 8F class   103
2–6–0 5MT class No 2700   88
2–6–0 5MT class No 42968   98
4–6–0 5MT class   99
4–6–0 'Jubilee' class   101
4–6–0 'Royal Scot' class   89
4–6–2 'Princess' class   98
4–6–2 'Coronation' class   105
2–6–4T 4P class No 2500   100
2–6–4 4MT class   111
2–6–0 4MT class   112
2–6–0 2MT class   111
2–6–2T 2MT class   112
Diesel shunter   97

London & North Eastern
4–6–2 A3 class   83
4–6–2 A4 class   102
4–6–2 A2 class   114
4–4–0 D49 class   91
2–6–2 V2 class   103
2–6–0 K4 class   104
2–6–0 K1 class   115
4–6–0 B1 class   108
Sentinel shunter   90

London, Tilbury & Southend
4–4–2T Thundersley   70

London Transport
0–6–0PT class   94

Mersey
0–6–4T Cecil Raikes   37

Metropolitan
4–4–0T No 23   18
0–4–4T No L44   52
Electric locomotive   67

Midland
2–4–0 No 158A   20
4–2–2 No 118   41
4–4–0 No 1000 (Compound)   63
0–6–0T No 1708   28
0–6–0 4F class   73

North British
4–4–0 *Glen Douglas*   76
0–6–0 *Maude*   72
0–4–0ST No 68095   42

North Eastern
2–2–4T *Aerolite*   22
2–4–0 Fletcher No 910   29
2–4–0 Tennant No 1463   37
4–4–0 Wordsall No 1621   49
0–6–0 J21 class   40
0–6–0 J27 class   70
0–8–0 Q6 class   75
0–8–0 Q7 class   79
0–6–0T J72 class   57
0–4–0T No 1310   43
Electric No 26500   63

Northern Counties Committee (LMS)
4–4–0 No 74 *Dunluce Castle*   86
2–6–4T No 4   112

North London
0–6–0T No 2650   40

North Stafford
0–6–2T No 2   65
0–4–0 Battery   78

Oxford & Aylesbury Tramroad
0–4–0T Aveling & Porter   25

Port Talbot
0–6–0ST No 813   62

Powlesand & Mason Ltd
0–4–0ST No 6   69

Ravenglas & Eskdale
2–8–2 *River Esk*   84
0–8–2 *River Irt*   90

Romney, Hythe & Dymchurch
0–4–0 No 4 *The Bug*   168

Shropshire & Montgomeryshire
0–4–2T *Gazelle*   50

Sligo, Leitrim & Northern Counties
0–6–4T   116

Somerset & Dorset
2–8–0 7F class   76

South Eastern & Chatham
4–4–0 Wainwright No 737   61
0–4–4T Wainwright No 263   67
0–6–0 Stirling No 65   52
0–6–0 Wainwright No 592   60
0–6–0T Wainwright   71

Southern
4–4–0 'Schools' class   94
4–6–0 'King Arthur class   88
4–6–0 'Lord Nelson' class   87
4–6–0 S15 class   90
4–6–2 'Battle of Britain' class   110
4–6–2 'Merchant Navy' class   107
4–6–2 'West Country' rebuilt   124
0–6–0 Q class   106
0–6–0 Q1 class   108
2–6–0 U class   91
0–6–0T USA class   109

Stockton & Darlington
Locomotion No 1   8
No 25 *Derwent*   13
0–6–0 No 1275   27

Taff Vale
0–6–2T   54

Talyllyn Railway
0–4–0ST No 1   19
0–4–0WT No 2   19
0–4–0WT No 6   79

Wantage Tramway
0–4–0WT *Shannon*   16

War Department
0–6–0ST Austerity   163
2–8–0 Austerity   109
2–10–0 Austerity   110

Welsh Highland
2–6–2T *Russell*   69

Welshpool & Llanfair
0–6–0T   64

West Clare
0–6–2T No 5   48